Parishes, Tithes, and Society
in Earlier Medieval Poland
c. 1100—c. 1250

TRANSACTIONS

of the

American Philosophical Society

Held at Philadelphia for Promoting Useful Knowledge

VOLUME 83 Part 2

Parishes, Tithes and Society In Earlier Medieval Poland c. 1100–c. 1250

Piotr Górecki

Assistant Professor of History
University of California, Riverside

THE AMERICAN PHILOSOPHICAL SOCIETY

Independence Square, Philadelphia

1993

Library of Congress Catalog
Card No.: 92-75294
International Standard Book No.: 0-87169-832-3
US ISSN: 0065-9746

To Renata and Ania,
with love

CONTENTS

Maps

ACKNOWLEDGMENTS

This essay originated during research and writing of my doctoral dissertation, "Economy, Society, and Lordship in Early Medieval Poland," completed at the Department of History of the University of Chicago in June 1988 under the guidance of Richard Hellie, now published by Holmes & Meier. I would like once again to acknowledge Professor Hellie's extraordinary help as dissertation supervisor, and as a model of scholarship, teaching, and collegiality. The dissertation, the resulting book, and the present work have benefitted immensely at every stage from close scrutiny and critique by Robert Bartlett, ever since his arrival at Chicago. I owe him an enormous debt for years of engaged and exciting association, and join in a loud chorus of regrets at his departure from my Alma Mater. Previous versions of this essay were presented at the Workshop in Medieval History at the University of Chicago, and at the Medieval Studies Workshop at University of California, Riverside. I owe thanks to Julius Kirshner, Richard Helmholz, and Ronald Inden at the University of Chicago, and to Brian Copenhaver, Richard Godbeer, Scott Martin, Robert Patch, Ralph Hanna, Conrad Rudolph, and Dericksen Brinkerhoff at the University of California, Riverside, for providing a context of critique and collegiality for my work. I am especially grateful to Robert Hine, who read an early version of this essay. I would also like to acknowledge the support of the American Council of Learned Societies for its generous subsidy of the dissertation from which this work emerged. I also thank Linda Bobbitt, Steve Walag, and Michael Capriotti of UCR Photographic/Illustration Services for producing the maps and the cover photograph. As always, I thank my parents, Danuta and Jan Górecki, in more ways than I can say; and dedicate this work to Renata and Ania, as a modest token of all they have given me.

INTRODUCTION

Tithes, parishes, and society in a dynamic context:
problems and approaches

Shortly after New Year of 1226, Pope Honorius III took steps to resolve a festering conflict between the duke of Silesia, Henry I the Bearded, and the bishop of Wrocław, the see of that duchy. The conflict had lasted for at least ten years, and may have reached back to 1207, the year of Lawrence's elevation to the episcopate. In 1226, Honorius ordered Bishop Lawrence to "abstain from inflicting unowed damage" on the duke.[1] Should Lawrence disobey the mandate, the pope appointed two German prelates from the nearby diocese of Meissen as judges delegate with instructions to cajole or compel the two parties to reach a settlement.[2] As expected, the bishop disobeyed; the following year, the judges noted that "dissension in the matter had been beyond measure," and that, with considerable difficulty, they convinced Henry and Lawrence to reach a compromise. They recorded the terms of that compromise in a detailed document.[3]

In his letter to the judges delegate of 1226, Honorius noted Henry's allegation that the bishop had subjected the inhabitants of his duchy to "unowed exactions levied as tithes," which were as he put it "contrary to the custom of the land observed by neighboring bishops."[4] Lawrence had demanded new tithe payments from "men who wish to inhabit the forests and other unsettled places . . . and bring them under cultivation."[5] As a

---

[1] *S.U.*, 1: no. 261 (1226), 191. For this conflict, see Tadeusz Silnicki, *Dzieje i ustrój Kościoła katolickiego na Śląsku do końca w. XIV* [The history and structure of the Catholic Church in Silesia through the end of the fourteenth century] (Warsaw, 1953), 146–53.

[2] Ibid. For the comparative background on papal judges delegate, see Richard Helmholz, "Canonists and Standards of Impartiality for Papal Judges Delegate," in Richard Helmholz, *Canon Law and the Law of England* (London, 1987), 21–40; Jane Sayers, *Papal Judges Delegate in the Province of Canterbury, 1198–1254* (Oxford, 1971); James Ross Sweeney, "Innocent III, Canon Law, and Papal Judges Delegate in Hungary," in James Ross Sweeney and Stanley Chodorow (eds.), *Popes, Teachers, and Canon Law in the Middle Ages* (Ithaca, 1989), 26–52.

[3] Ibid., no. 281 (1227), 207.

[4] Ibid., no. 261 (1226), 191.

[5] Ibid.

1

result, "not only are they reluctant to settle and cultivate these places, but those who have come to cultivate [them] leave and move to other regions because of the hardships that befall them."[6] The depopulation led to political complications. "As a result, the places remain deserted, the borderlands of the duchy are occupied, and grave conflicts . . . arise between him and the neighboring nobles into whose lands his settlers move."[7] Duke Henry had alleged a devastating impact of Lawrence's demands on settlement in his duchy, on his authority over its inhabitants, and implicitly on the entire social, economic, and political order over which he presided.

In his complaint to the pope, Duke Henry may have exaggerated the seriousness of the consequences alleged against the bishop. It is difficult to imagine that new settlement and rural expansion in fact came to something near the grinding halt suggested by Henry's complaints as a result of the tithes asserted by the bishop. Quite apart from the degree of the alleged harm, the allegation of that particular harm sheds some light on the dynamics of peasant migration into and within the duchy. Under Lawrence's predecessors, new inhabitants had been migrating into Silesia in substantial numbers, and expanding rural settlement and arable. Once they were deterred by the new payments, inhabitants migrated into structures of highly articulated power. After abandoning Henry's authority, they routinely resettled under the "nobles." Whoever the "nobles" were, they recruited inhabitants of the duchy in sufficient numbers to cause conflicts with Henry. They actively competed for these inhabitants; thus, this society had experienced competition for labor since at least 1207. The turn of the century was thus an expansionary period of clearing and settlement in the duchy and diocese. This expansion was also underway in the dioceses neighboring Wrocław and thus can securely be generalized to at least a substantial part of western and southern Polish provinces.

Overall, then, on the face of the record the letter of 1226 appears to reflect a society in demographic and economic transition, and refers vaguely to one group with a distinct degree of power in society, the "nobles." Movement of inhabitants into and within the duchy, competition for labor among the duke and "nobles," and land clearing, all suggest that the thirteenth century was a period of expansion of the population, of intensive

---

[6]Ibid.
[7]Ibid.

land clearing, and of a proliferation of forms of tenure and lord-ship that accompanied these processes.[8] The words of Duke Henry's complaint repeated by Pope Honorius appear to situate the duchy in the broad context of expansion of arable and settle-ment underway in medieval Europe throughout the later elev-enth, twelfth, and most of the thirteenth centuries.[9] They also situate the duchy among the regions of medieval Europe in which migration of settlers from other regions played an important role in these processes. In this sense, Honorius's letter appears to refer to a medieval European frontier in dynamic transition.[10] The document compiled by the judges delegate the following year supplements these general impressions, fills in the broad pic-ture of fluidity and change with a wide variety of statuses and specializations of the inhabitants, and not least important de-flates the rhetorical thrust of systemic demise alleged by the duke and passed on by the pope.

In its general contours, the controversy recorded in 1226 and 1227 resembles conflicts between secular and ecclesiastical pos-sessors of tithe revenue throughout Europe in the central Middle Ages. Nominally, the tithe was a tenth of all revenues of the me-dieval economy, intended for support of the priesthood; in prac-tice in the course of the Middle Ages tithe payments refracted into a wide range of practices affecting possession, assessment, gathering, and consumption of revenues, a wide range of lay and ecclesiastical control over these areas, all against a background of intense and detailed conflict.[11] By the early thirteenth century, all

---

[8]On these subjects, see Piotr Górecki, *Economy, Society, and Lordship in Medieval Po-land, 1100-1250* (New York, 1992); for an analysis over a far larger sweep of time and with a different emphasis, see Richard C. Hoffmann, *Land, Liberties, and Lordship in a Late Medieval Countryside: Agrarian Structures and Change in the Duchy of Wrocław* (Phila-delphia, 1989).

[9]Marc Bloch, *Feudal Society*, trans. by L. A. Manyon (Chicago, 1961); Georges Duby, *La société aux XIᵉ et XIIᵉ siècles dans la région mâconnaise* (Paris, 1953, 2nd ed. 1971). Duby's suc-cessors include: Pierre Toubert, *Les structures du Latium médiéval: le Latium méridional et la Sabine du IXᵉ siècle à la fin du XIIᵉ siècle* (Rome, 1973); Jean-Pierre Poly, *La Provence et la société féodale (879–1166): contribution à l'étude des structures dites féodales dans le Midi* (Paris, 1976); Robert Fossier, *La terre et les hommes en Picardie jusqu'à la fin de XIIIᵉ siècle* (Paris and Louvain, 1968); idem, *Enfance de l'Europe, Xᵉ-XIIᵉ siècles: aspects économiques et sociaux* (Paris, 1982).

[10]For the frontier problem and Eastern Europe in its context, see Robert Bartlett and Angus MacKay (eds.), *Medieval Frontier Societies* (Oxford, 1989), especially the articles by Paul Knoll, "Economic and Political Institutions on the Polish-German Frontier in the Mid-dle Ages: Action, Reaction, Interaction" (151–76), Alfred Thomas, "Czech-German Rela-tions as Reflected in Old Czech Literature" (199–216), Friedrich Lotter, "The Crusading Idea and the Conquest of the Region East of the Elbe" (267–306), and Robert I. Burns, "The Significance of the Frontier in the Middle Ages" (307–30).

[11]James Brundage, "Tithes," in Joseph Strayer (ed.), *Dictionary of the Middle Ages*, 12: 62–65; Giles Constable, *Monastic Tithes from their Origins to the Twelfth Century* (Cambridge, 1964), 16–19, 34–35, 97, 114–15, 114–26, 134–36.

these features of tithing had long been subjects of general and regional ecclesiastical legislation, litigation, and canon law. One result has been a number of schemes allocating possession and consumption to revenues among bishops, parish priests, and other recipients, and the concomitant role of the bishops in the disposal of tithe revenues in favor of particular tithe possessors.[12] Another result was exemption of particular types of clergy from obligation to pay tithe, and their own acquisition of its possession. Monasteries in particular enjoyed both exemption from, and possession of, tithe from their estates, with specific arrangements made for the new monastic orders of the twelfth century, especially the Cistercians.[13] Finally, possession and control over tithe were adapted to local practices of lordship and tenure. Obligations to pay tithe varied according to the status of goods tithed, and whether they were products (in a nominal sense) of the land or of other factors of production. Hence exemptions of tithe obligations of the portions of estates held in demesne; adjustments of tithe obligations from newly cleared arable; variations in the assessment of personal, praedial, and mixed tithes; and distinction between the great tithe, payable in grain, and small tithe, payable in a wide range of other economic products.[14] All these areas of legal concern reflected generations of economic, demographic, tenurial, and seigneurial transformation throughout Europe, and the broad contours of adaptation of tithe to that transformation.

Within these broad and standardized contours of ecclesiastical law and practice, tithing régimes varied in different regions of Europe. These issues, conflicts, and their resolutions offer insight into the structure of the societies and economies of which tithes were an aspect.[15] The content of tithe obligations, the process of tithe payment, the units of settlement subject to tithe, and variation in these areas over time and space all shed light on the economy and demography of the society subject to tithes. Patterns of possession of tithe, ability to gather and disburse tithe revenue, and control over the flow and disposal of tithe revenue reflect differences in power and status among different categories of laymen and ecclesiastics who were involved in the collection

---

[12]Brundage, "Tithes," 63; Constable, *Monastic Tithes*, 27, 40–48, 51–56, 126–27.

[13]Constable, *Monastic Tithes*, 242–49, 279.

[14]Brundage, "Tithes," 64; Constable, *Monastic Tithes*, 4, 34, 105–06, 235–37, 287–88, 294–95.

[15]A superb study of adaptation of the assessment, levying, collection, and disposal of tithes to a regional economy is Catherine E. Boyd, *Tithes and Parishes in Medieval Italy: The Historical Roots of a Modern Problem* (Ithaca, 1952).

and consumption of tithe, and in the gifts of tithe revenue. Transfers of tithe revenue among ecclesiastical possessors reflect the power of various categories of clergy with respect to disposal and possession of tithe.

Grants of tithe revenue to particular churches were also an important step in the establishment of networks of spiritual care. Endowment of churches with tithe revenue frequently accompanied their elevation to parish status, that is, a grant of "cure of souls" (*cura animarum*), including the right to administer sacraments and instruction in orthodox dogma and conduct to some community of the faithful.[16] Although possession of tithe revenue was not a formal defining element of that status, tithe possession and parish status were related formally and in practice. Despite wide variation in actual patterns of its control and possession of tithe revenue in the Middle Ages, support for parish clergy remained the formal purpose of tithe.[17] Since the Carolingian period, creation of parishes was usually accompanied by a gift of tithe revenue.[18] Thus, in conjunction with other information, grants of tithe revenue constitute circumstantial evidence on the formation of parishes.

Throughout Europe, this process occurred in a broad demographic, economic, and institutional context. Churches provided spiritual care over a variety of units or regions of settlement, ranging from central places to individual localities; their records therefore provide sensitive evidence of demography and patterns of settlement.[19] Churches also provided differing areas of spiritual care, especially over time. Older churches in a particular region gradually hived off most of their spiritual functions in favor of new foundations in the regions they serviced. The process occurred differently in different parts of Europe, but its common feature was a diffusion and localization of spiritual care,

---

[16]This working definition of the parish is based on Michel Aubrun, *La Paroisse en France des origines au XVe siècle* (Paris, 1986), 18, 34–36, 59–67, 96); Richard E. Sullivan, "Parish," *Dictionary of the Middle Ages*, 9: 411–17, at 411; Colin Morris, *The Papal Monarchy: The Western Church from 1050 to 1250* (Oxford, 1989), 296–97; Reynolds, *Kingdoms*, 81. The second part of the working definition is somewhat problematic; by it, I mean merely that a particular church appears to have served a congregation not limited to a group of clergy or an entourage of a ruler, at a level of certainty comparable to that inferred in other regions of Latin Europe. Beyond that, this study does not focus on the structure and religiosity of that "community," partly because of conceptual disagreements about what constitutes communities, and partly because of the scarcity of the relevant evidence.

[17]Constable, *Monastic Tithes*, 85–87, 100–03, 126–28.

[18]Aubrun, *La Paroisse*, 44, 88–92, 126–33.

[19]Duby, *La société*, 231, n. 43.

and subdivision of large parishes into smaller units.[20] Since the process was related, among other things, to population expansion, it sheds further light on demographic change. It also documents the relative power of central and local clergy, and thus the balance of power within regional ecclesiastical institutions.[21]

Like tithe revenues, churches were subject to a wide range of secular and ecclesiastical control. Rulers and other powerful laymen all asserted degrees of control over endowment, construction, consecration, and staffing of churches at all levels of spiritual and administrative responsibility. Powerful laymen recurrently subjected local churches to lordship and, to use a slightly anachronistic term, "privatized" them.[22] In much of Western Europe, this process elicited reform aimed at restoring ecclesiastical independence from secular control, in the restitution of parish churches by ecclesiastical authority, and in acquisition of control over a substantial proportion of these churches by the regular clergy.[23] This in turn led to controversy and conflict over administration of spiritual care between secular and regular clergy, and among the different orders of the latter. Tracing these changes was an enormous corpus of canonical, conciliar, and synodal legislation concerning the relative spheres of competence of different categories of clergy, formal control of these spheres of competence by prelates, popes, and legates, and formal rights of

---

[20]Aubrun, *La Paroisse*, 18–22, 33–36, 39–42, 70–76, 108–13; John Blair, "Introduction," in Blair (ed.), *Minsters and Parish Churches: The Local Church in Transition, 940–1200* (Oxford, 1988), 1–16; Morris, *Papal Monarchy*, 60, 294–97; J. M. Wallace-Hadrill, *The Frankish Church* (Oxford, 1983), 286–88; Christopher Brooke, "Rural Ecclesiastical Institutions in England: The Search for Their Origins," *Settimane di studio del Centro italiano di studi sull'alto medioevo*, 28 (Spoleto, 1982): 685–711, at 690–91, 695–705; Robert Fossier, *Enfance de l'Europe* (Paris, 1982), 1: 346–58; Susan Reynolds, *Kingdoms and Communities in Western Europe, 900–1300* (Oxford, 1984), 78–100, at 81–90.

[21]Note, for example, Reynolds's remarks on variations in what she calls the "two-tiered" parish structure, using Italy and England as examples, in *Kingdoms*, 82–85.

[22]Aubrun, *La Paroisse*, 69–78; Wallace-Hadrill, *Frankish Church*, 286; Morris, *Papal Monarchy*, 60–61; Richard E. Sullivan, "Parish," in Joseph Strayer (ed.), *Dictionary of the Middle Ages*, 9: 411–17, at 412. In the analysis that follows, I generally avoid the terms "private" and "proprietary" because I consider them anachronistic, and especially distorting for comparative synthesis of Polish parishes in the European context.

[23]Aubrun, *La Paroisse*, 78–88; Morris, *Papal Monarchy*, 60–61, 171–72, 221–22, 253–54, 390–91; John Van Engen, *Rupert of Deutz* (Berkeley-Los Angeles, 1983), 327, n. 94; Guy Devailly, "Le clergé régulier et le ministère paroissial," *Cahiers d'histoire*, 20 (1975): 259–72; Joseph Avril, "Paroisses et dépendances monastiques au moyen âge," in *Sous la Règle de Saint Benoît: structures monastiques et sociétés en France du moyen âge à l'époque moderne* (Geneva, 1982), 95–106; idem, "Recherches sur la politique paroissiale des établissements monastiques et canoniaux (XIe-XIIIe siècles)," *Revue Mabillon*, 59 (1980): 453–513; Giles Constable, "Monastic Rural Churches and the *cura animarum* in the Early Middle Ages," *Settimane di studio del Centro italiano di studi sull'alto medioevo*, 28 (Spoleto, 1982): 349–89; Robert Somerville, " 'Pope Clement in a Roman Synod' and Pastoral Work by Monks," *Monumenta Germaniae Historica*, Schriften, Bd. 33. II (Hanover, 1988), 151–56; Ursmer Berlière, "L'exercice du ministère paroissial par les moines dans le haut moyen âge," *Revue Mabillon*, 39 (1927): 227–50.

patronage over churches by the clergy and the laity. The results measure the relative power of different kinds of clerics and laymen in different regions of Europe.

Variations of these features of the medieval law and practice are especially interesting in those regions of medieval Europe that experienced rapid changes in settlement, economy, lordship, and institutions around the turn of the thirteenth century. One such region was the Polish duchies comprising the archdiocese of Gniezno.[24] The later twelfth and much of the thirteenth centuries were a period of rapid change in the ecclesiastical and social structure of medieval Poland, and in the amount of documentation of that change. The decades spanning the Fourth Lateran Council were a time of intensive reform of religious practice, belief, institutions, and their relationship to secular power by prelates of the archdiocese, with active support of popes, papal legates, and papal judges delegate.[25] It was also a period of proliferation of local churches in the archdiocese, and of their association with parochial status.[26] During this period, the written sources illustrating the development of parishes and tithes become sufficiently ample and diverse to shed light on distinctive regional patterns, and to situate these patterns in a broader comparative perspective.[27] The details trace out the specificities

---

[24]This is the region to which I refer interchangeably as "Poland" and "Polish duchies," and whose inhabitants and institutions I qualify with the adjective "Polish." I mean to imply no anachronistic national meanings to these terms; I also recognize that their use poses special problems in analyzing categories of inhabitants their contemporaries considered ethnically distinct, especially Germans and Jews. For a particularly careful and non-anachronistic definition of "Poland" as a historical construct, see Norman Davies, *God's Playground: A History of Poland* (New York, 1982), 1: 23–105. The other major works in English include: Oskar Halecki, *A History of Poland* (New York, 1943); Francis Dvornik, *The Slavs in European History and Civilization* (New Brunswick, 1962); Paul Knoll, *The Rise of the Polish Monarchy: Piast Poland in East Central Europe, 1320–1370* (Chicago, 1972); Aleksander Gieysztor (ed.), *History of Poland*, 2d ed. (Warsaw, 1979); Antoni Mączak, Henryk Samsonowicz, and Peter Burke (eds.), *East-Central Europe in Transition: From the Fourteenth to the Seventeenth Century* (Cambridge and Paris, 1985); and, most recently, Richard Hoffmann's monumental *Land, Liberties, and Lordship*.

[25]For the implementation of the provisions of the ecumenical councils of the thirteenth century in the archdiocese of Gniezno, see Bolesław Kumor and Zdzisław Obertyński (eds.), *Historia Kościoła w Polsce* [History of the Church in Poland], vol. 1, pt. 1 (Poznań-Warsaw, 1974), 112–24, 143–51; Józef Szymański, "Biskupstwa polskie w wiekach średnich: organizacja i funkcje" [Polish dioceses in the Middle Ages: organization and functions], in Jerzy Kłoczowski (ed.), *Kościół w Polsce* [The Church in Poland] (Kraków, 1966), 1: 127–236, at 129–48; Silnicki, *Dzieje*, 148–49, 159–64, 309–24; Adam Vetulani, *Statuty synodalne Henryka Kietlicza* [The synodal statutes of Henryk Kietlicz] (Kraków, 1938).

[26]Eugeniusz Wiśniowski, "Rozwój organizacji parafialnej w Polsce do czasów reformacji" [Development of the parish organization in Poland until the Reformation], in Kłoczowski, *Kościół*, 1: 237–372, at 263–69; Silnicki, *Dzieje*, 85–88, 356–61.

[27]The periodization of the eleventh, twelfth and earlier thirteenth centuries as the "earlier" Middle Ages in Poland is conventional among Polish historians. The evidence of tithes and parishes from this period matches the evidence of several other areas of the social, legal, political, and economic order in medieval Poland. These areas include,

of the ecclesiastical institutions and practices of this region, and the integration of the region into the cultural orbit of medieval Europe.

A study of parish churches in earlier medieval Poland confronts several difficulties. Even in the most richly documented regions of medieval Europe, identification of status of particular churches, of their origins, of their institutional relationships to other churches, and of the precise range of their spiritual functions is often difficult and sometimes calls for educated guesses.[28] The problems are compounded by recurrent ambiguity of the terminology pertaining to units of spiritual care and the clergy involved in administering it. In different places and at different times, the terms *parochia, parochianus, sacerdos, plebs, plebanus, capella,* and *capellanus* referred to different types of churches, units of spiritual care, and ecclesiastical offices, and so are not an adequate guidance to the range of spiritual functions or degree of localization of the churches and offices to which they refer, especially in absence of other evidence.

These conceptual difficulties become especially acute in a region of Europe that experienced christianization and the appearance of written record quite late, and thus suffers from the dearth of written record at the outset of its political, religious, and institutional history.[29] Written evidence appears late and is modest

---

among others: politics, kingship, the economy, the patterns of settlement, towns and countryside, the legal system, religiosity and religious institutions. Details of the periodization vary, but there is general consensus that the earlier period in the Middle Ages ends sometime at or after the mid-thirteenth century. For the periodization of the Polish medieval history, see among others Karol Modzelewski, *Organizacja gospodarcza państwa piastowskiego, X-XIII wiek* [The economic organization of the Piast state from the tenth to the thirteenth century] (Warsaw, 1975); Modzelewski, *Chłopi w monarchii wczesnopiastowskiej* [The peasants in the early Piast monarchy] (Wrocław, 1987); Henryk Łowmiański, *Początki Polski* [The origins of Poland] (Warsaw, 1963–73), vol. 6; Marek Cetwiński, *Rycerswo śląskie do końca XIII wieku: pochodzenie, gospodarka, polityka* [Silesian knighthood through the end of the thirteenth century: origins, economy, politics] (Wrocław, 1980); Jerzy Mularczyk, *Władza książęca na Śląsku w XIII wieku* [Ducal power in Silesia in the thirteenth century] (Wrocław, 1984); Oskar Kossmann, *Polen im Mittelalter: Beiträge zur Sozial- und Verfassungsgeschichte* (Marburg/Lahn, 1971); Kossmann, *Polen im Mittelalter: Staat, Gesellschaft, Wirtschaft im Bannkreis des Westens* (Marburg/Lahn, 1971); Davies, *God's Playground*, 61–91; from a later perspective, Hoffmann, *Land, Liberties, and Lordship*, 16–21; Knoll, *Rise*, 1–13.

[28]For some of the conceptual difficulties of identifying parish churches, see J. H. Bettey, *Church and Parish: An Introduction for Local Historians* (London, 1987), 15–17, 22–24.

[29]Zygmunt Sułowski, "Początki Kościoła polskiego" [Beginnings of the Polish Church], in Kłoczowski, *Kościół*, 1: 17–123; concerning the use of the written document, see Karol Maleczyński, *Dyplomatyka wieków srednich* [Medieval diplomatics] (Warsaw, 1971), 122–27, 140–46; idem, "Rozwój dokumentu polskiego od XI do XV wieku" [Development of the Polish document from the eleventh through the fifteenth centuries], in Karol Maleczyński, *Studia nad dokumentem polskim* [Studies on the Polish document] (Wrocław, 1971), 242–76, at 242–50.

thereafter. There is virtually no information about local churches and their function for at least two hundred years after the conversion of Duke Mieszko I in 966; the "origins" of parishes in Poland are therefore entirely inaccessible. Evidence becomes richer in the twelfth and thirteenth centuries, which is the period under study. Though rudimentary, it offers teasing glimpses of social and institutional complexity. The scarcity and lateness of the evidence seriously complicate study of early ecclesiastical institutions in their social and political context in this region of Europe. It is difficult to assess which elements of the picture are routine and typical, which are important, and which represent continuity or innovation.

The difficulty has pushed the students of the earliest Polish ecclesiastical and spiritual history in three directions. One is to focus the inquiry on institutions primarily on the issue of their origins, and specifically on the likelihood of the existence of parish churches in appreciable quantity in the archdiocese of Gniezno for three centuries before there is any written evidence about them.[30] Another is to reduce institutions along with other areas of economy and society to some one, supposedly paradigmatic element and source of order, such as exceptionally strong power of the rulers in the establishment of parish churches in the tenth and eleventh centuries and exceptionally strong power of lords in their establishment in the twelfth and thirteenth.[31] A third is to assume a general systemic delay of all institutions in this region, and to explain the appearance and proliferation of parishes as essentially a late and weak diffusion into a frontier region of Europe.[32]

---

[30]This is one of the polemical cruxes of the otherwise superb pioneering studies of the parishes in early Poland, posing the work of Julia Tazbirowa and Heinrich Felix Schmid against the work of Eugeniusz Wiśniowski and several others. Julia Tazbirowa, "W sprawie badań nad genezą organizacji parafialnej w Polsce" [Research on the origins of the parish organization in Poland], *Przegląd Historyczny*, 5 (1963): 85–92; eadem, "Początki organizacji parafialnej w Polsce" [Origins of the parish organization in Poland], ibid., 369–86; Wiśniowski, "Rozwój," 239–56; Heinrich Felix Schmid, *Die rechtlichen Grundlagen der Pfarrorganisation auf westslavischen Boden und ihre Entwicklung während des Mittelalters* (Weimar, 1938); this book is a reprint of a monograph under the same title published in five very long segments in the *Zeitschrift der Savigny-Stiftung für Rechtsgeschichte, Kanonistische Abteilung*, of which the segments dealing primarily with Poland are: 17 (1928): 264–358, and 18 (1929): 285–562.

[31]Modzelewski, *Organizacja*, chapter 1; Aleksander Gieysztor, "Le fonctionnement des institutions ecclésiastiques rurales en Bohême, en Pologne et en Hongrie aux Xe et XIe siècles," *Settimane di studio del Centro italiano di studi sull'alto medioevo*, 28 (Spoleto, 1982): 927–30, 934–36, 940, 942–45; Aubrun, *La Paroisse*, 69.

[32]Colin Morris treats most of the topics associated with the institutional Church in Eastern Europe in a separate, and relatively late, chapter on "the Christian frontier," despite the fact that some relevant processes might be more intelligible in their contemporary context. Morris, *Papal Monarchy*, 263–77.

All these responses are plausible and potentially fruitful, but each risks serious distortion. The search for "origins" of parishes in Poland is saddled with lack of evidence and with some intrinsic conceptual ambiguities. Authors who engage in the controversy do not clearly state whether the controversy concerns the earliest appearance of churches that provided spiritual care, or the time when such churches constituted a network aimed at, and accessible to, groups that can be described as communities of the faithful. Supporters of the early appearance of a parish network, or "organization," point to the earliest churches situated in the major fortified centers of the Polish duchies, which included episcopal, monastic, royal, and comital churches; argue that such churches must have offered spiritual care; and consider them, taken together, as a parish network. The difficulty with this view is that the social functions of these churches cannot be ascertained. They must have offered spiritual services to someone, but it is not clear to whom and with what effect. It seems impossible simply to assume that they serviced communities of the faithful outside small royal and ecclesiastical groups, and perversely skeptical simply to assume that they did not, at some time or other during the three centuries after Duke Mieszko.

To reduce control over churches and their revenue to royal, seigneurial, or indeed any other single power threatens unnecessary simplification and stereotyping, particularly in a region of Europe that has recurrently been subject to both.[33] To be sure, the rulers and lords controlled all kinds of churches, but as far back as the documentation extends they shared that control with ecclesiastics in complex and meaningful ways. Finally, a presumptive treatment of large regions of Eastern Europe as an unambiguous borderland into which institutions and practices diffuse in a familiar but delayed rhythm obscures the fact that

---

[33]For the sources and expressions of traditional comparative approaches of Eastern and Western Europe in the Middle Ages, as well as for their revisions, see: Hermann Aubin, "Medieval Agrarian Society at Its Prime: The Lands East of the Elbe and German Colonisation Eastwards," in Michael M. Postan (ed.), *The Cambridge Economic History of Europe* (2nd ed., Cambridge, 1966), 1: 449–86; Richard Koebner, "The Settlement and Colonisation of Europe," ibid., 1: 1–91; Lynn White, Jr., *Medieval Technology and Social Change* (Oxford, 1962), 41–57; Georges Duby, *Rural Economy and Country Life in the Medieval West*, tr. by Cynthia Postan (Columbia, S.C., 1968), 17–18; Pounds, *An Economic History*, 195–96; Graeme Barker, *Prehistoric Farming* (Cambridge, 1983), 159–60. Meitzen's assumptions respecting medieval Europe in general have been alternately revised and re-accepted, in ebbs and flows shaped by both World Wars and by the intellectual implications of decolonization among European and American scholars. An important revision is underway right now. For the historiography of this subject, see Górecki, "Economy, Society, and Lordship in Early Medieval Poland," Ph.D. dissertation (University of Chicago, 1988), 1–154; Górecki, *Economy*, 1–9.

some of the processes glimpsed through Polish documentation seem directly comparable to exactly contemporary processes elsewhere in Europe, others occur later, and others have no documented counterparts at all. Through the evidence for Poland, we glimpse processes comparable to those of other regions of Europe, but not in any rhythm that lends itself to convincing periodization. Ducal and seigneurial control over parish churches and their revenues, monastic appropriation of both, emergence of a parish network, ecclesiastical attempts at reform of all these areas and to carve out areas of institutional and economic autonomy, are all documented continuously throughout the twelfth and thirteenth centuries. Thus, the notable feature of this region is strictly speaking not a time lag, but a specific integration of interrelated processes, resulting in distinct patterns of power and control within this society.

This study avoids the questions of "origins" altogether. It concerns itself instead with the period in which parish churches and tithe revenues are explicitly documented, and disavows the debate about how far back that documentation can in some sense be projected. It does, however, attempt to identify those features of local churches and tithing that were routine, innovative, and controversial at the time the documents were produced; and to assess directions of change during the period of documentation. Thus, while the "origins" of these institutions in an absolute sense are inaccessible, a relative chronology of tradition, routine practice, and innovation can be established. The study also does not use any particular source of initiative—royal, seigneurial, papal, monastic, imperial, or popular—as a logical anchor for the institutional "origins" of particular institutions, but rests on a working assumption that in the earliest period local churches were founded and endowed through collective initiatives from several sources. Finally, it disavows the treatment of Poland as an undifferentiated frontier zone, and begins with a working assumption that the processes that took place there are potentially comparable to those that characterized Western Europe, but subject to a different periodization and with distinct results. None of these working assumptions is "provable," or intended as a proxy voice in the relevant debates. However, they ought to be useful for reassessing the available evidence on its own terms.

The work consists of two parts, each of which is treated in two chapters. The first part focuses on parishes, the second on tithes. Chapter 1 begins with a short treatment of the earliest, exceedingly skeletal, evidence of the initiatives behind the foundation of local churches, of their endowment with parochial status,[34] and of the patterns of territorial and social control associated with them. The rest of the chapter situates the foundation of local churches and their elevation to parish status in the context of economic and demographic expansion in the Polish duchies, with special emphasis on Silesia. The resulting analysis does not pretend to trace out a full parish network, but it does reconstruct the social and economic dynamics of parish expansion, and briefly sets that reconstruction in comparative perspective. Chapter 2 analyzes parishes from a different perspective. It focuses on patterns of control over local and parish churches in the archdiocese of Gniezno and the clergy that staffed them. It examines control by bishops through archdeacons and archpriests, by dukes and other powerful laymen through foundation, patronage, and threats of violence, and control by monastic communities through appropriation and its consequences. The conflicts, competition, and compromises over control for parish churches and their clergy add up to distinctive patterns of ecclesiastical and secular power within this society.

Chapters 3 and 4 concern primarily tithes. They examine all the groups involved in the possession, production, gathering, alienation, and consumption of tithes in the Polish society of the twelfth and earlier thirteenth centuries, as far as the evidence allows. Chapter 3 examines the clerical groups involved in alienation of tithe revenue. Most of the documented recipients of tithe revenue are monastic communities and the parish churches appropriated by them. The tithe revenues are usually alienated by cathedral canons and priests of the appropriated parishes, with their consent. The authoritative transfer is always made by the bishop and chapter. Evidence of transfers of tithe revenues to local churches is therefore a sensitive measure of the relationships among different categories of clergy, especially bishops, the chapter, individual canons, monastic communities, and parish priests.

Chapter 4 examines the secular groups involved in alienation of tithe revenue, both actively and passively, in the archdiocese of Gniezno. It reconstructs the tithe obligations to which different categories of inhabitants of the Polish duchies were subjected,

---

[34]As used here, "local church" means any church that is neither the seat of a bishop nor a cloister, and that cannot be identified as a parish church. A "parish church" means a local church that has been elevated to parochial status, as defined earlier. This working definition is not entirely satisfactory, but fortunately the Polish contemporaries were quite clear about what they meant by parish churches and by the spiritual care they delivered.

and the tithe obligations from which certain categories were exempted. It also examines patterns of control over the disposal and gathering of tithe revenue that defined privilege in Polish society, and situates these patterns in a contemporary tenurial context. It especially notes the emergence of Polish knighthood as a privileged group in the context of tithes.[35] Finally, it traces out changes in these patterns over time. The patterns reflect continuity and change in the economy and demography of the Polish duchies, and to that extent Chapter 4 complements the analysis of Chapter 1. They also provoke conflict; the resulting competition for tithe revenues and compromise reflects the relative strength of several categories of laity and clergy in this society. These conclusions of Chapter 4 complement the analysis of Chapter 2.

Evidence

The essay rests on several kinds of evidence: episcopal and ducal charters, papal bulls and letters, verdicts by papal legates and judges delegate, statutes of synods and councils held before Polish bishops and papal judges, and narrative sources. Between them, this documentation records grants of tithe revenues, areas of settlement and economic activity subject to tithes; resolutions of conflicts over assessment, collection, and consumption of tithes; records of local churches and definition of their status, accounts of the formal spiritual care that these churches performed, records of monastic and secular power over parishes and their clergy, conflicts in all of these areas, and their resolutions.

Three narratives are the earliest sources relevant to local churches and their spiritual function in Poland. One is an account written before 1018 by the German bishop of Merseburg, Thietmar, in which the author comments on what might be called the ethical structure of the Polish society, and the role of clerical and secular authority in its formulation and enforcement.[36] The

---

[35]For comparison of the statuses of *miles* throughout various parts of Europe in the central Middle Ages, see, among others: Sally Harvey, "The Knight and the Knight's Fee in England," in Rodney Hilton (ed.), *Peasants, Knights and Heretics: Studies in Medieval English Social History* (Cambridge, 1976), 133–76; C. Warren Hollister, *The Military Organization of Norman England* (Oxford, 1965), pp. 58, 115–16, 121; Georges Duby, "The Nobility of Medieval France," in Georges Duby, *Chivalrous Society*, tr. by Cynthia Postan (Berkeley-Los Angeles, 1977), 94–111, at 103–08; Benjamin Arnold, *German Knighthood, 1050–1300* (Oxford, 1985); John B. Freed, "Nobles, Ministeriales and Knights in the Archdiocese of Salzburg," *Speculum*, 62 (1987): 575–611, at 579–97.

[36]*M.P.H.*, 1: 230–322, with the relevant passage at 311–12.

second is a letter from Pope Gregory VII to the Polish king, Bolesław II the Bold, written in 1075 to admonish the king to help establish a parish network in his kingdom.[37] The third is a brief sketch by the anonymous chronicler conventionally known as Gallus of the initiatives behind the foundation of local churches in Poland just after the turn of the twelfth century, in the midst of narrating the early deeds of his patron Duke Bolesław III.[38] Information yielded by these sources is exceedingly fragmentary, but in conjunction with later evidence they help anchor the narrative, and offer a partial substitute for the inaccessible "origins."

In general, sources from the earlier twelfth century remain sparse and laconic. The most important early source is the bull issued by Pope Innocent II in 1136 to the archdiocese of Gniezno.[39] The bull includes a survey of a large estate granted to the archdiocese throughout the Polish duchies. Tithes are among the components of this estate recorded in the survey. These components are recorded with reference to the largest, fortified centers of settlement, production, and defense, the large roundworks (or systems of roundworks) usually called *castra*, made of earth, stone, and wooden palisades on massive infrastructures, and the regions around them.[40] The survey included in the bull

---

[37]*M.P.H.*, 1: 367–68.

[38]*M.P.H.*, 1: 449, lines 1–26.

[39]Edition used: Stefan Vrtel-Wierczyński, *Wybór tekstów staropolskich: czasy najdawniejsze do roku 1543* [A selection of Old Polish texts: from the earliest times through 1543] (4th ed., Warsaw, 1969), pp. 1–8. This source is hereafter cited as *V.-W.* Since the lines of this document are indicated consecutively over the full eight pages, not page by page, I cite passages from it by lines alone. For diplomatic analysis and issue of authenticity, see Karol Maleczyński, "W sprawie autentyczności bulli gnieźnieńskiej z r. 1136" [Concerning the authenticity of the Gniezno bull of 1136], in Karol Maleczyński, *Studia nad dokumentem polskim* (Warsaw, 1971), 170–88. His skepticism has been rejected in the literature, as noted by Stanisław Płaza, *Źródła drukowane do dziejów wsi w dawnej Polsce: studium bibliograficzno-źródłoznawcze* [Printed sources for the history of the village in Old Poland: a bibliographic and source study] (Warsaw-Kraków, 1974), 42, n. 96.

[40]For the political and economic functions of these fortified cores of settlement, see: Modzelewski, *Organizacja*, 92–135; idem, "Jurysdykcja kasztelańska i pobór danin prawa książęcego w świetle dokumentów XIII w." [The castellan's jurisdiction and the collection of taxes due according to ducal law in light of thirteenth-century documents], *Kwartalnik Historyczny*, 87 (1980): 149–73; Tadeusz Wasilewski, "Poland's Administrative Structure in Early Piast Times," *Acta Poloniae Historica*, 44 (1981): 71–99; Aleksander Gieysztor, "En Pologne médiévale: problèmes du régime politique et de l'organisation administrative du Xe au XIIIe siècles," *Annali della fondazione Italiana per la storia amministrativa*, 1 (1964): 135–56. For the relationship between "castles" and tithes specifically in Silesia, see Walter Kuhn, "Kastellaneigrentzen und Zehntgrenzen in Schlesien," *Zeitschrift für Ostforschung*, 21 (1972): 201–47, reprinted in Walter Kuhn, *Neue Beiträge zur schlesischen Siedlungsgeschichte: Eine Aufsatzsammlung* (Siegmaringen, 1984), 12–49. See also Lucien Musset, *Les invasions: le second assaut contre l'Europe chrétienne (V^e-XIe siècles)* (Paris, 1965), pp. 95–96, and Eric Fügedi, *Castle and Society in Medieval Hungary* (Budapest, 1986), 15–41.

Map 1. Important Centers of Settlement in 1136 and 1227

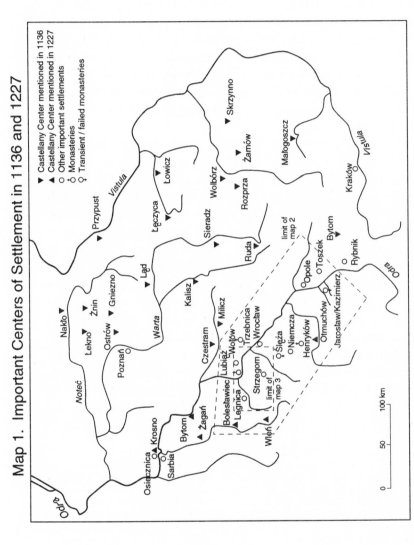

▼ Castellany Center mentioned in 1136
▲ Castellany Center mentioned in 1227
○ Other important settlements
○̕ Monasteries
♀ Transient / failed monasteries

Source: *Atlas Historyczny Polski* (Warsaw, 1977), pl. 6-III

alternately describes each of these territorial centers as "the city (*civitas*) and all passages around the city and around . . . the adjacent castles (*castella*)," and more simply as "the castles (*castella*) . . . and the places adjacent to them."[41] The terms *civitas* and *castellum* appear to be used interchangeably. Whatever the term used, the grid of the survey is the Polish variant of the earlier medieval town.[42] One of the provisions specifies the tithes due to the archdiocese from the territories and the satellite settlement around each town. This document is an informative overview of the content of tithes and the economy from which they are due, but contains no information either on the specific allocation of tithe obligations, or any particular churches supported by the tithes.

The written evidence becomes more detailed after the fourth decade of the twelfth century. Much of it consists of records of endowment of the diocese of Wrocław and of several monastic communities with estates between the third decade of the twelfth century and for at least one century thereafter. The monastic communities were all situated within a radius of about fifty kilometers around Wrocław. Thus, this body of evidence pertains to a local region within the Polish duchies.[43] The endowments are recorded in charters issued by dukes and bishops. Among other components of estates, the charters record local churches and tithe revenues that have been acquired from prior possessors. Two of the monastic recipients of local churches and tithe revenues were situated in Wrocław itself, that is, a few hundred meters from the fortified center that was the earliest place of settlement in the city.[44] These were two houses of Augustinian canons regular of St. Mary's and St. Vincent's, established in the earlier twelfth century and reformed in subsequent decades.[45]

---

[41]*V.-W.*, lines 22–23, 85–90; the two lists are included in lines 18–23 and 85–90.

[42]For the definition of towns in the earlier Middle Ages, see Robert Fossier, *Enfance de l'Europe* (Paris, 1982), 2: 980–1047, and, for Slavs, ibid., 1035–38.

[43]In this work, I shall repeatedly refer to this region as "central Silesia," as the "relatively well-documented region," or with some plainly intelligible equivalent. For a superb introduction to that region, see Hoffmann, *Land, Liberties, and Lordship*, 13–22; also Silnicki, *Dzieje*, p. 3, n. 1.

[44]For the area of settlement that comprised Wrocław in the earlier Middle Ages, see Marta Młynarska-Kaletynowa, *Wrocław w XII-XIII wieku: przemiany społeczne i osadnicze* [Wrocław in the twelfth and thirteenth centuries: social and settlement changes] (Wrocław, 1986); Andrzej Wędzki, "Wrocław," in *Słownik Starożytności Słowiańskich*, 6: 604–14. For identification of the places in the town district of Wrocław, see the editors' indices to *S.U.*, and Józef Domański, *Nazwy miejscowe dzisiejszego Wrocławia i dawnego okręgu wrocławskiego* [Place-names of today's Wrocław and the former district of Wrocław] (Warsaw, 1967).

[45]Silnicki, *Dzieje*, 93, 97–108, 369–71 377–79; Wędzki, "Wrocław," 606.

In addition, three Cistercian communities were endowed in the region in the later twelfth and earlier thirteenth centuries. The Cistercian houses of Lubiąż and Trzebnica were situated fifty and twenty kilometers to the northwest and north of Wrocław respectively. They were founded between the 1160s and 1218. Finally, the Cistercian monastery at Henryków was founded and endowed between 1222 and 1228 about sixty kilometers to the south of Wrocław.[46]

The type and breadth of evidence pertaining to local churches, tithes, and parishes in Poland changed during the pontificate of Innocent III, and after the Fourth Lateran Council in 1215. The years preceding the Council, and the half-century or so afterwards, were marked by a rise in activity by the archbishops of Gniezno, other Polish bishops, and papal legates and judges delegate in order to reform and regulate tithing practices and the activities and staffing of local churches in all the Polish dioceses. Early in 1207, Innocent III wrote a series of short letters to the Polish clergy, dukes, and laity concerning the state of the Church in Poland.[47] A recurrent theme of these letters is control by laity over the selection and maintenance of the clergy, at the expense of episcopal authority. The letters constitute a deliberate and systematic effort at reform; five were issued on the same day, the sixth one day after, and the seventh three days after the sixth. Innocent's initiative was a part of the broad current of ecclesiastical reform in different regions of Europe in the years preceding the Fourth Lateran Council.[48] Sometime after 1207, Bishop Lawrence demanded the standardized, canonical tithes from the inhabitants of the duchy, thus leading to conflict with Duke Henry. The conflict produced rich documentation in the papal mandate to the judges delegate, in their verdicts, and other records.[49]

Polish bishops and papal legates held a series of reforming synods between 1233 and 1267. Detailed synodal legislation was issued by Archbishop Pełka in 1233, by the papal legate James of Liège in 1248, by Bishop Thomas of Wrocław between 1248 and 1254, again by Archbishop Pełka in 1257, by Archbishop Janusz in

---

[46]*S.U.*, 1: no. 45 (1175), 26–28; no. 83 (1202–03), 54–58; no. 93 (1204), 63–66; no. 115 (1208), 80–85; no. 143 (1215), 101–02; no. 171 (1218), 123–26; no. 271 (1226), 199; no. 290 (1228), 213–14; 2: no. 38 (1233), 26–27; no. 103 (1235), 66–68. Silnicki, *Dzieje*, 108–18, 381–87; Wacław Korta, *Rozwój wielkiej własności feudalnej na Śląsku do połowy XIII wieku* [The development of feudal great property in Silesia until the mid-thirteenth century] (Wrocław, 1964); for Henryków in particular, see Heinrich Grüger, *Heinrichau: Geschichte eines schlesischen Zisterzienserklosters, 1227–1977* (Cologne-Vienna, 1978).
[47]*S.U.*, 1: no. 102–09 (1207), 73–77.
[48]Morris, *Papal Monarchy*, 533–34.
[49]*S.U.*, 1: no. 153 (1217), 111; no. 261 (1226), 191; no. 281 (1227), 206–07.

1262, and by the papal legate Guido in 1267.[50] The resulting statutes address all the issues Innocent III had raised at the outset of
the century, most notably questions of control over parish
churches and parish priesthood, and conflicts concerning the
rights and obligations in tithes. The synodal statutes implemented ecumenical church reform, and adapted the provisions of
the reform to the tithing practices routine in the Polish duchies.
Some of these documents referred to the Fourth Lateran Council,
either as a time after which a conflict over ecclesiastical matters
must be resolved canonically, or as a source of substantive rules
for resolving a conflict or altering a practice.[51] During the same
period, episcopal charters and papal letters addressed problems
of competition among several categories of clerics for control over
parish churches, selection of their clergy, and the administration
of spiritual care.[52]

Finally, two narrative sources refer to several categories of
clergy, including parish priests, bishops, and monks. One is a
chronicle of the Cistercian monastery of Henryków in southern
Silesia.[53] This document consists of three parts. The first two
parts are histories of all the monastic acquisitions in the district
around the monastery since its foundation into the authors' own
time. The first part was written in the 1270s, the second in the
early fourteenth century. The author of the first part was almost
certainly Peter, the fourth abbot of the monastery, while the identity of his continuator is unknown. The third part is a catalog
of the bishops of Wrocław from the origins of the diocese until
the last third of the thirteenth century.[54] Its authorship is also
unknown, but its writing is contemporary with Abbot Peter's

---

[50]*S.U.*, 2: no. 34 (1233), 20–23; no. 346 (1248), 204–16; 3: no. 182 (1248–57), 125–26; no. 246 (1257), 162–63; no. 416 (1262), 275–76; *K.Wp.*, 1: no. 423 (1267), 370–75. Silnicki, *Dzieje*, 310–22; for an excellent study of Legate Guido in the context of thirteenth-century coun-cils, see idem, "Kardynał legat Gwido, jego synod wrocławski w roku 1267 i statuty tego synodu" [Cardinal legate Gwido, his Wrocław synod of 1267, and the statutes of this synod], in idem, *Z dziejów Kościoła w Polsce: studia i szkice historyczne* [Fragments of the his-tory of the Church in Poland: studies and historical sketches] (Warsaw, 1960), 321–80.

[51]*S.U.*, 1: no. 281 (1227), 207 (a tempore concilii Lateranensis); 2: no. 34 (1233), 22, line 41 (secundum constitutionem concilii Lateranensis).

[52]Ibid., no. 60–61 (1193), 37, 40; no. 156–57 (1217), 113–14; 2: no. 397 (1250), 252, lines 26–28; 3: no. 89 (1253), 67, lines 42–44.

[53]Roman Grodecki (ed.), *Księga henrykowska. Liber fundationis claustri sancte Marie Virginis in Heinrichow* (Poznań-Wrocław, 1949). Hereafter cited as *K.H.* A superb treatment of the authorship and context of the first book of the chronicle is Józef Matuszewski, *Najstarsze polskie zdanie prozaiczne: zdanie henrykowskie i jego tło historyczne* [The oldest Polish sentence in prose: the sentence of Henryków and its historical background] (Wrocław, 1981).

[54]*K.H.*, chaps. 197–211, pp. 371–82. On the lists of bishops of Wrocław, their textual origins and transmission, and their reliability, see Roman Heck, "The Main Lines of Development of Silesian Medieval Historiography," *Quaestiones Medii Aevi*, 2 (1981): 63–87 at 65, n. 9.

narrative. The other source is a Life of St. Hedwig of Bavaria, wife (later widow) of Duke Henry the Bearded of Silesia, and an important initiator of his monastic foundations, especially the convent of Trzebnica.[55] It was written by an unknown hagiographer shortly after 1300.

These sources were produced after the period under study, and are reconstructions of past events. I use them rather sparingly, and in conjunction with more contemporary evidence. I draw on the first book of the Henryków chronicle and on the bishops' list; the events relevant to tithes, parishes, and clergy narrated in these two sources are removed from the time of the writing by about thirty years at most, are sometimes almost contemporary, and explicitly within easily accessible memory and witness. The events narrated in the hagiographic source are more distantly removed from the author's present, and also more stereotypical; I therefore use only a single passage in which the hagiographer portrays several categories of clergy in a way that meshes with much earlier evidence, and in which the bias inherent to this type of source enhances rather than diminishes the quality of his information on that particular subject.

---

[55] *M.P.H.*, 4: 501–655; on this remarkable woman, and on the challenges of the hagiographic genre through which she is best known, see: Teresa Wąsowicz, "Une légende silésienne: sainte Hedwige dans la tradition littéraire et iconographique du XIIIᵉ siècle," in Pierre Gallais and Yves-Jean Riou, *Mélanges René Crozet* (Poitiers, 1966), 2: 1073–78; Joseph Gottschalk, *St. Hedwig, Herzogin von Schlesien* (Cologne-Graz, 1964); André Vauchez, *La sainteté en Occident aux derniers siècles du moyen âge d'après les procès de canonisation et les documents hagiographiques* (Rome, 1981), 432–33; Donald Weinstein and Rudolph M. Bell, *Saints and Society: The Two Worlds of Western Christendom, 1000–1700* (Chicago, 1982), 90.

1. PARISHES, TITHES, AND ECONOMIC EXPANSION

Local churches, tithes, and parish formation in the twelfth century

In his view from afar of the archdiocese of Gniezno, Pope Innocent II was self-consciously solicitous. "With apostolic care and authority," he expressed concern for "the region of the Poles, situated in the farthest parts of the world," and for its pastor, Archbishop James.[56] The distant view telescoped and distorted the image of that region conveyed by the document of 1136. Neither the survey compiled by Archbishop James nor the comments appended to it in the papal chancery refer to any kind of ecclesiastical structure in the archdiocese of Gniezno. Nothing is said about either episcopal or local churches, or about the clergy; and nothing is even implied about the relationship between churches, clergy, and the rest of the population. Of course, his silence does not mean that no ecclesiastical institutions existed; the century and a half preceding 1136 were in fact the formative period of the Polish episcopate and monasticism in Poland, and a period of intensive christianization. Innocent's concern is less significant for any reality to which it might refer—this is largely inaccessible—but as a theme in terms of which the earliest available written sources construct religious life in Poland. The few commentators from other regions of Europe who turn their attention to the subject at all express a recurrent perception of the inadequacy and peripherality of Polish ecclesiastical institutions and their social function between the eleventh and thirteenth centuries, harmful to the welfare of this faraway people.[57]

Paradoxically, two statements in this vein constitute our earliest written evidence on these subjects. From their very different points of view, Thietmar of Merseburg and Pope Gregory VII both note an institutional vacuum in the society on which they

---

[56]*V.-W.*, lines 5–8.

[57]A brilliant treatment of this type of problematic in a later period is Andrzej Feliks Grabski, *Polska w opiniach Europy Zachodniej, XIV-XV w.* [Poland in Western European opinion in the fourteenth and fifteenth centuries] (Warsaw, 1968).

are reflecting.[58] Thietmar alleged an absence of institutional structure to motivate the Poles towards religiously proper behavior without terror. "Since divine law," noted Thietmar, "has only recently appeared in these parts," the Poles are "compelled" to observe a religious custom "by power rather than by fasts imposed by bishops."[59] The custom consisted of abstaining from meat consumption for an unusual length of time during the year; the *potestas* behind it was extraordinarily brutal punishment. "Whoever is found to eat meat after Lent is severely punished by having his teeth knocked out."[60] Thietmar did not explicitly say who carried out the punishment, but, in another general gloss on the state of the Poles, implied that the agent was the king. "The people" of the kingdom "have to be fed like cattle, and disciplined in the fashion of sluggish donkeys; and cannot be engaged for the prince's welfare without severe punishment."[61]

The area of social discipline on which Thietmar focused was sexual misconduct, for which the Poles inflicted on each other a wide array of horrific punishment. Two areas of sexual misconduct called for punishment that was not only extraordinarily painful but also very public. Both involved promiscuity by married persons; both entailed removal of the offending organ; one was directed at men, the other at women. The gravamen of the offense by men was intercourse with married women. The males offended by "using the wives of another," with them, suggesting that the offended parties were husbands of the unfaithful women.[62] A woman was punished "if found to be a prostitute (*meretrix*)."[63] In both cases, the punishment was mutilation of the genitals. Both men and women were punished in public places— the men at "the market bridge" (*pons mercati*), the women "at the doors" (*in foribus*) presumably of their homes.[64] The author emphasizes the deliberate deterrent effect of these penalties.[65]

Thietmar commented on the details of these punishments with unmitigated horror—though in suspiciously rich detail—and from a clearly hostile point of view; he may have exaggerated

---

[58]*M.P.H.*, 1: 311–12, 367–68.
[59]*M.P.H.*, 1: 312, lines 4–7.
[60]Ibid., lines 2–4.
[61]Ibid., 311, lines 24–27.
[62]Ibid., lines 27–29.
[63]Ibid., 312, line 26. What kind of behavior Thietmar characterized as *meretrix* or thought the Poles of the eleventh century did is unclear. For a general comparative context as of the early eleventh century, see James A. Brundage, *Law, Sex, and Christian Society in Medieval Europe* (Chicago, 1987), 147–48.
[64]*M.P.H.*, 1: 311, line 30312, lines 1–2, 26–31.
[65]Ibid., 312, lines 29–31.

their frequency, immediacy, inflexibility, and effectiveness. His focus on sexuality is commonplace medieval idiom of critique of exotic societies; but his observation that sexual offenses were deliberately punished in public places offers a plausible glimpse into some features of sanction of private behavior that ought to be independent of his strong dislike towards the Poles and their kings. The society on which he reflected was subject to a fairly well-articulated system of control of social practices affecting private conduct at the turn of the tenth and eleventh centuries.[66] This system operated in public places; it was based in the central places in which exchange took place, or which experienced especially heavy traffic related to exchange. Thus, whatever we may think about the real severity of that system, it rested on a territorial network, and was therefore routine. Absent from Thietmar's narration is any personnel, clerical or otherwise, involved in the enforcement of the social norms among the Poles. After his brief assertion that Poles did not fear their bishops, he simply presented the elaborate penal maimings as a kind of impersonal horror, a constitutive element of a repulsive social order.

Writing from a very different perspective fifty years later, Pope Gregory VII also noted an absence of ordinary ecclesiastical structure in the kingdom of Bolesław II. He noted with regret "that among such a multitude of people there are so few bishops, and the dioceses (*parochiae*) of each are so large that the cure of the episcopal office can in no way be carried out or properly administered in the subject localities (*subiectis plebibus*)."[67] Gregory's complaint clearly called for a division of large territorial units of spiritual care, the *parochiae*, under authority of bishops who were unable to perform it properly, into smaller units, the *plebes*. His concern and the terms he used for the larger and smaller units of spiritual authority correspond exactly to the processes of division of large *parochiae* into networks of parishes throughout medieval Europe between the Carolingian period and the eleventh century.[68]

Perhaps because of the successive crises of the first Polish kingdom, concern with the structure and social function of the Polish

---

[66]See on this subject Jerzy Dowiat, *Chrzest Polski* [The baptism of Poland] (Warsaw, 1969), 144–46; Sułowski, "Początki," 117; Gieysztor, "Le fonctionnement," 935.

[67]*M.P.H.*, 1: 368, lines 3–7.

[68]For Western Europe, see, among others, Aubrun, *La Paroisse*, 18–22, 33–42, 48–49, 68–78; John Blair, "Introduction: From Minster to Parish Church," in John Blair (ed.), *Minsters and Parish Churches: The Local Church in Transition, 940–1200* (Oxford, 1988), 1–19; Reynolds, *Kingdoms*, 81–90; for the terminology in the legislation of Hungarian kings, see Eugeniusz Wiśniowski, "Rozwój," *Kościół*, 1: 237–372, 263–69.

Church utterly disappears from the written record until the turn of the thirteenth century. In the bull of 1136, Innocent II concerned himself solely with the composition of tithes, and with the main Polish centers of population with their satellite settlements on which the tithe revenues were imposed. The northerly group of "cities" was granted to the archdiocese with[69]

full tithes in grain, in honey, and in iron, in [revenue from] taverns [and from] trials (*placita*), in marten and fox pelts, in pigs, [and] in tolls [collected] within the city itself and throughout all the passages to the city (*tam in ipsa civitate quam per omnes transitus civitati*), that is [throughout] the . . . adjacent castles (*castella*).

The other group of fortified centers was granted with an identical tithe list, except that it explicitly included tithes "from the markets" (*de foris*), which, like the rest, were to be collected "in the castles (*castella*) themselves, and in all places (*loca*) adjacent to them, by every passage (*per omnes transitus*)."[70] The tithes were imposed on a wide gamut of products, economic activities, and legal processes. The imposition of tithes on a variety of potentially taxable activities, ranging from grain to profits of justice, shows that Archbishop James and Pope Innocent intended to subject a broad range of lucrative economic activities to tithes. The plan to subject the widest possible spectrum of social production to tithes corresponds to the formal canonical injunction that all products and revenues in society must be tithed.[71]

The content of the tithes and the territory from which they were due show the broad patterns of economic production and exchange in the archdiocese of Gniezno. The demanded content indicates that the rural output included agriculture, mineral extraction, hunting for small animals (whose skins were perhaps used as a medium of exchange), exercise of jurisdiction, and trade. The manner in which the tolls were planned indicates the geography of that trade. The tolls were placed on all the "passages" between any "city" and its fortified satellite settlement points, presumably smaller versions of the centers. The "cities" or "castles" were therefore hubs of local and regional trade, and central parts of a hierarchy of settlement, defense, and exchange places (markets). Each fortified center was a core of a hierarchy; the satellite *castella* were its intermediate zones; and the other

---

[69]Ibid.
[70]Ibid.
[71]Constable, *Monastic Tithes*, 16–19, 102–04.

places of settlement (*loca*) not referred to in these opening lists at all, but termed *villae* elsewhere in the survey were its interstitial third tier.[72] The passages (*transitus*) between the central and intermediate places in the exchange hierarchy were understandably the places in which tolls on trade could be established relatively conveniently.

The earliest glimpse of local churches in this large territorial structure is the brief passage in which the anonymous chronicler known as Gallus described the establishment of local churches in Poland during the first two decades of the twelfth century, and thus around the time when Archbishop James compiled the survey included in the bull of 1136.[73] In the midst of narrating the early deeds of his patron Duke Bolesław III, Gallus noted that "a certain noble built a church within the boundaries of the land, and invited Duke Bolesław at that time a boy with his [fellow] youths to its consecration."[74] Almost immediately after the consecration, the noble used the new church for a wedding. Gallus bitterly disapproved of this conjunction of consecration and marriage, and noted that a similar practice had led to madness and misfortune for priests and newlyweds "at the consecration of the church of Ruda."[75]

Brief as it is, Gallus's vignette records several features of the foundation of the church that he considered standard in Polish society. The church was established by a "noble." Gallus did not define the meaning of "nobility," but clearly implied that "noble" status was privileged; it enabled its holder to serve as host to the ruler and his companions at the consecration of the church he built, and at the subsequent wedding. Gallus's didactic tone against the consequences, and his use of a specific church as an example, suggests that he saw these practices as routine. "Nobles" must have established churches frequently, and consecrations of these churches were significant gatherings for a variety of political and spiritual purposes.[76] At the outset of the twelfth century, therefore, formation of new churches was a complex of initiatives among three parties: the "noble" who initiated the foundation, the ruler who was present at the attendant ritual,

---

[72]The role of the fortified centers conforms to the model of intermediate and long-distance exchange proposed by Richard Hodges in his study of the economy of early medieval Europe; see Richard Hodges, *Dark Age Economics: The Origins of Towns and Trade, A.D. 500–1000* (London, 1982), 13–25.

[73]*M.P.H.*, 1: 449, lines 1–26.

[74]Ibid., lines 10–14.

[75]Ibid., lines 1–2, 15–16, 25–26.

[76]Gieysztor, "Le fonctionnement," 945.

and the cleric who consecrated the church. Schematic as it is, Gallus's list of participants recurs in the documentation in the
twelfth and thirteenth centuries. The documents illustrate the
range of meanings of Gallus's "noble," the formal relationship of
that figure to dukes, and the roles of the clergy in the foundation
and consecration of local churches, and in the definition of their
spiritual functions.

Ever since Gallus wrote, secular landholders either founded
churches on their estates, or conveyed them among other endowment and sources of revenue. Around the time Pope Innocent II
issued the bull for the archdiocese of Gniezno, a substantial land-
holder in central Silesia named Peter Włast and his relatives built
and conveyed several churches in the region to two new communities of canons regular in Wrocław. In or shortly before 1139 Peter "built" a cloister of St. Mary's in Wrocław, and a "chapel"
(*capella*) of St. Michael beside it.[77] "Bogusław, lord Peter's brother,
gave the church of St. Adalbert," situated just south of the fortified center of Wrocław; and Cieszebór, "lord Peter's relative,"
granted several other nearby settlements.[78] During the next
ten years, the family granted two more capellae to the community, and "lady Włast" (*comitissa Vlostonissa*)—evidently Peter's
mother—added another village.[79] In 1149 or 1150, some years after Peter's death, Bishop Walter of Wrocław identified Peter, his
wife Mary, and his son Świętosław as the primary benefactors of
the community of the canons regular, while in 1193 Pope Celestine III described him as one of the "patrons of the place."[80] Peter's reputation as a founder of churches increased in the
generations after his death; he was remembered as a founder of
over seventy individual churches, including monastic foundations and churches of lesser status.[81]

The trickle of information on secular possession and convey-
ance of churches continues throughout the twelfth and early thirteenth centuries. In his record of 1198 of the acquisitions of the
Hospitaller house in Miechów, the monastic author notes that
"lord Radosław gave us Skaryszów with the church, market, and
tavern for his soul," and that "lord Mikora gave Chełm with the
church."[82] In 1217, Duke Henry attested to a Zachary, son of

---

[77] *S.U.*, 1: no. 19 (1139–49), 15.
[78] Ibid., no. 23 (1149–50), 18; no. 59 (1193), 35.
[79] Ibid.
[80] Ibid., no. 58 (1180–1201), 35.
[81] *M.P.H.*, 2: 3, lines 19–20; 520, lines 6–25.
[82] *K.Maz.*, no. 142 (1198), 134, lines 24–25; no. 143 (1198), 139, lines 1–2, 5–6.

Hartwig, granting "his village of Zachowice with the church of that village" to the diocese of Wrocław.[83] Four years later, Bishop Lawrence granted tithe revenues to "the church of lord Andrew" situated in one locality, on the occasion of the consecration of "the church of lord Werner" in another.[84] Finally, in 1233 a land-holder named John, son of Sibota, made a last will in which he left to some of his descendants "my village of Pransina, in which lord Thomas, bishop of Wrocław, has founded a church in honor of blessed Peter the Apostle."[85] He compiled the document "in my village of Pransina, on the day on which the said bishop founded the church in the said village."[86]

Two individuals, father and son, were closely associated with church foundation in the later twelfth century and the first years of the thirteenth. Their case offers a glimpse into the relationship between the "noble," ducal, and episcopal roles in ecclesiastical endowment at the turn of the twelfth and thirteenth centuries. Sometime between 1201 and 1203, Emmeram, son of Gniewomir, confirmed his gift of "the church of Strzegom with its appurte-nances" to a new community of the Hospitallers near Wrocław.[87] The church at Strzegom was quite old at this time. In his confir-mation of Emmeram's gift a few days later, Bishop Cyprian noted that the church had been consecrated by his predecessor, Walter, sometime before 1149.[88] The secular founder of the church must have been Emmeram's father Gniewomir. Gniewomir and Em-meram had long enjoyed a close relationship with Dukes Bole-sław the Tall and his son Henry the Bearded. Gniewomir coop-erated with both dukes in endowing the monastery of Lubiąż. Duke Bolesław gave Gniewomir an important settlement called Ujazd, which Gniewomir in turn granted to the monks of Lubiąż between 1175 and 1202. Emmeram confirmed his father's gift be-fore Duke Henry in 1202.[89] At this time, he was an official of Duke Henry. In his charter for the Lubiąż monks of 1202, Henry called him "my baron and castellan."[90]

The relationship of dependence between the two families con-tinued. In 1202 and 1203, Duke Henry asserted an active and for-mal role in Emmeram's gift to the Hospitallers. He was present at

[83]S.U., 1: no. 159 (1217), 115.
[84]Ibid., no. 240 (1223), 175.
[85]Ibid., 2: no. 32 (1233), 18, lines 41–42.
[86]Ibid.
[87]Ibid., no. 86 (1201–03), 60.
[88]Ibid., no. 88 (1203), 61.
[89]Ibid., no. 77 (1202), 50.
[90]Ibid.

Emmeram's grant of the church in Strzegom to the Hospitallers; Emmeram recorded him first among the witnesses in the charter he issued concerning the gift.[91] In his own confirmation of Emmeram's gift, Henry referred to Emmeram as "my noble" and "castellan of Ryczyn," and stressed his own "consent and permission" to Emmeram's gift.[92] A few months later, Bishop Cyprian reiterated Henry's consent in his own grant of tithe revenue to the church.[93] Thus, although in his charter Emmeram portrayed himself as donor to the of church of St. Peter's, Duke Henry on his side asserted charge over Emmeram and the church at Strzegom, and the bishop duly complied with that view.

The dukes also played significant roles in the transfers of tithe revenues, though they always acknowledged the formal role of bishops in the foundation of churches and in the endowment of the churches with tithe revenues. Whenever the dukes recorded transfers of tithe revenue, they attributed them to the bishops of the see in which the transfer was effected.[94] They occasionally, however, shared control over tithe revenues. In his charter of 1175 for the monks of Lubiąż, Bolesław the Tall noted "I and the bishop of Wrocław, Żyrosław," granted the monks tithe revenue from villages to be established in the district of Legnica.[95] In 1206, his son Henry acquired from the canons regular of St. Vincent's the place called "Oława with two churches, the right to gather tithe, and all the revenues" in exchange for another holding.[96] Nothing else is known about the two churches in Oława, but it is clear that as a result of the exchange they and their revenues accrued to ducal possession and presumably ducal control.

Fragmentary as they are, these glimpses offer insight into a systematic enforcement of private ethical conduct based on specific localities and public sanction at the outset of the eleventh century, a plan to integrate the population that experienced this enforcement into a network of parishes in the later eleventh century, the sources of initiative in the establishment of local churches in the early twelfth century and thereafter, and a plan to gather tithe revenues from what appears to be the society as a whole in the third decade of the twelfth century. This insight is, of course, extremely limited. The eleventh-century sources in

---

[91]Ibid., no. 86 (1201–03), 60.
[92]Ibid., no. 87 (1203), 60.
[93]Ibid., no. 88 (1203), 61.
[94]Ibid., no. 19 (1139–49), 15; no. 45 (1175), 28; no. 83 (1202–03), 57; no. 115 (1208), 82–83; K.Maz., no. 143 (1198), 139, lines 5–9.
[95]S.U., 1: no. 45 (1175), 28.
[96]Ibid., no. 101 (1206), 73.

particular are exceedingly difficult to situate in a broader spiritual or institutional framework; they do suggest, however, the territorial units of expression and control of collective belief that might have constituted a base for the earliest parish organization in Poland. This reading explains Gallus's perception of routine (if spiritually misguided) foundation of local churches in Poland in the early twelfth century.

The documents also shed some light on the initiators of ecclesiastical foundation. Gallus's vignette and the subsequent records underscore the secular role in foundation of local churches, and appear to confirm the view that in this region the earliest documented local churches were "private," seigneurial foundations.[97] While this particular synthesis is clearly not wrong, it seems misdirected. Scarce as they are, the records spanning Gallus's narrative of the unnamed "noble" and Emmeram, Henry, and Cyprian's accounts of the gift of the church at Strzegom, portray the establishment of new churches as essentially a collective activity involving three actors. The "noble" possessed the church and its appurtenances and initiated the foundation; the duke asserted authority over the "noble" and his holdings (including the church); the bishop approved these claims and retained the right to transfer tithe revenue. Within the group imagined by Gallus, the "noble" possessed limited but significant rights of initiative, and it is in this rather specific sense that his relationship to the church was "proprietary" or "private." However, in view of the collective initiative behind the formation of churches, I am a bit reluctant to attribute new church foundation in Poland, in some essential or paradigmatic sense, to one particular category of agents, whether secular or ecclesiastical; and to characterize the foundations as essentially ducal, seigneurial, "private," episcopal, or something else.

Expansion of parish churches, c. 1170–c. 1230: demographic and economic context

Aside from these fragmentary accounts, the twelfth century was a time of awkward documentary silence concerning any churches other than episcopal and monastic. This silence lasted until monastic churches began the long process of appropriation of local churches since the later twelfth century and well into the

---

[97] Aubrun uses Eastern Europe as a paradigmatic region of "private" parish churches; *La Paroisse*, 69.

thirteenth. The most important appropriating monastic communities included the Cistercian houses of Lubiąż, Trzebnica, and
Henryków, the houses of canons regular of St. Vincent's and St.
Mary's in Wrocław, a house of the Knight Hospitallers at Strzegom, and, somewhat later, the first mendicant priory established
in the province, the Dominicans of Wrocław.[98] The period of appropriation coincides with the episcopate of Lawrence, the pontificate of Innocent III, and the early years of the pontificate of
Honorius III, a period of intensive reform in the archdiocese of
Gniezno. The subsequent engagement of monastic communities
in the supervision and expansion of parishes may have been a regional counterpart of the earlier restitution of local churches from
secular to ecclesiastical control in Western Europe, and the resulting shift towards monastic patronage over local churches.[99] It
may also have been a compensation for the alleged inadequacy of
the Polish episcopate in implementing ecumenical policies that
papal and legatine documents occasionally express with various
degrees of impatience.

Appropriation is difficult to set in a broader context because we
do not have comparably detailed evidence on those local
churches that were not appropriated by the regular clergy; therefore we cannot directly assess the frequency of monastic appropriation, in Silesia or in the archdiocese of Gniezno in general. It
was in any event the best documented process affecting local
churches and their status in the region of Wrocław. Evidence of
monastic appropriation of local churches and their revenues extends back into the middle of the twelfth century, specifically the
episcopate of Walter. In 1218, Bishop Lawrence of Wrocław noted
that four of his predecessors had consented to appropriations by
the monks of Lubiąż of several previously existing churches and
their tithe revenues.[100] Lawrence's recollection corresponds to
the episcopate of Walter, who was remembered on several occasions as the consecrator of several local churches in the district
of Wrocław.[101] Lawrence's document of 1218 therefore nicely
brackets the history of the appropriated local churches over several generations.

---

[98]*S.U.*,1: no. 19 (1139–49), 15; no. 67 (1201), 48–49; no. 82 (1202), 54; no. 85 (1203), 59; no.
88 (1203), 61; no. 171 (1218), 123–26; no. 266 (1226), 195.

[99]Aubrun, *La Paroisse*, 78–85, 113–15.

[100]He confirmed for the monks "all the tithes of their church and of the churches that
pertain and are subject to it, which they have justly obtained at various times by the legitimate gifts of our predecessors of blessed memory, Walter, Żyrosław, Jarosław, and
Cyprian, and of ourselves." Ibid., no. 171 (1218), 124.

[101]Ibid., no. 19 (1139–49), 15. For Walter and his successors, culminating with Lawrence,
see Silnicki, *Dzieje*, 35–42, 49–57.

Map 2. Local Churches and Settlement in Silesia, 1202 and 1227

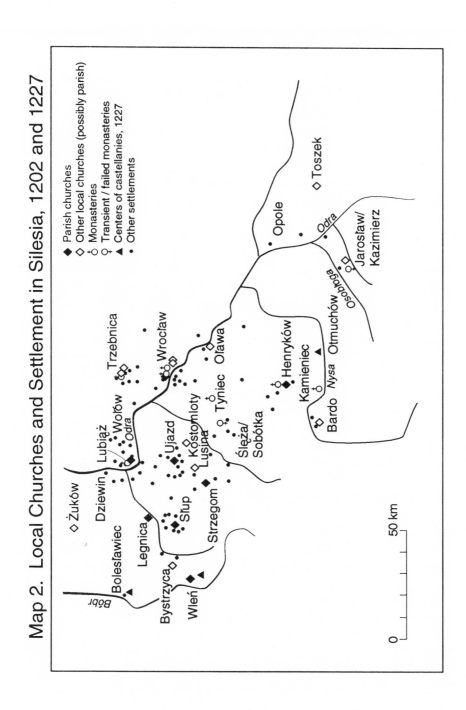

Legend:
- ◆ Parish churches
- ◇ Other local churches (possibly parish)
- ⚨ Monasteries
- ♀ Transient / failed monasteries
- ▲ Centers of castellanies, 1227
- • Other settlements

Żuków · Dziewin · Wołów · Trzebnica · Wrocław · Lubiąż · Odra · Ujazd · Kostomłoty · Lusina · Tyniec · Oława · Śleża/Sobótka · Henryków · Kamieniec · Bardo · Nysa · Otmuchów · Osobłoga · Opole · Odra · Jarosław/Kazimierz · Toszek

Bolesławiec · Legnica · Bystrzyca · Wleń · Słup · Strzegom · Bóbr

0   50 km

Monastic appropriation carried a wide range of possible consequences for the relationship between the appropriating institution and the appropriated local church. The monks acquired control over the endowment of the appropriated churches, including tithe revenue. Transfer of tithe revenues is the most frequent subject of the documents recording monastic appropriation of local churches.[102] They also acquired control over, and interest in, the spiritual functions of the appropriated local churches. The results depended on the status of the appropriated churches prior to appropriation, and the desire of the appropriating communities to maintain or enhance that status. The results varied. Some communities either did not adopt any particular policy regarding the spiritual functions of the churches they appropriated, or positively abandoned any such spiritual functions. Shortly before 1202, the Cistercian nuns acquired the parish church of St. Peter's in Trzebnica and its tithe revenue, but there is no record about the fate of that church, its spiritual functions, or the clergy that staffed it in the subsequent evidence.[103] The intended status of Lord Emmeram's church of St. Peter's in Strzegom after 1203 is unclear; presumably it was to serve the Hospitallers as their first cloister church.[104] The "old," wooden church that had existed in Henryków at the time the Cistercian monastery was founded between 1222 and 1227 was certainly a cloister church during the first phase of the existence of that community.[105]

Other communities, on the contrary, formalized the spiritual functions of the local churches they acquired and assumed formal supervision over them. They defined the parish status of the churches, traced out their boundaries, and sought to limit competition from other places of cult in the future. The three monastic communities that adopted these approaches included the Cistercian monastery at Lubiąż, and the communities of canons regular of St. Vincent's and St. Mary's in Wrocław. The monks of Lubiąż were actively supported by Bishop Lawrence in acquiring these functions. In 1217, he assigned "cure of souls" (*cura*

---

[102]S.U., 1: no. 19 (1139–49), 15; no. 67 (1201), 48–49; no. 82 (1202), 54; no. 85 (1203), 59; no. 88 (1203), 61; no. 171 (1218), 123–26. The appropriating communities also presumably acquired control over the livelihood and function of the clergy parochial or otherwise that staffed the appropriated church, although the records of appropriations by the three monastic communities are silent on that specific subject.

[103]Ibid., no. 83 (1202–03), 56.

[104]Ibid., no. 86–88 (1203), 59–61. See Silnicki, *Dzieje*, 119–20.

[105]K.H., chaps. 65–68, pp. 264–66.

animarum) to local churches within their estate, and recorded the boundaries of the resulting parishes.[106] He also anticipated formation of additional local churches within each parish, and sought to accommodate the rights of the four parish churches he had just created. "Any churches that arise within these boundaries in the future shall be daughters of [each] mother church, and the rights of the mother church shall be preserved in every way."[107] Each parish would in the future include a central church, the *ecclesia matrix*, and other churches with more limited rights and obligations of spiritual care.

The Wrocław houses of St. Mary's and St. Vincent's were protected in similar roles by papal bulls. At the turn of the twelfth and thirteenth centuries, Innocent III recorded seven local churches within the estate of St. Vincent's.[108] In 1193, Celestine III defined the holdings of St. Vincent's and St. Mary's as their *parochiae*, and prohibited construction of unauthorized new churches within them. He assured both communities that "no one may dare newly to build a chapel or an oratory within the boundaries of your *parochia* without assent by the bishop of the diocese and by you."[109] Innocent IV repeated this phrase word for word in his protective bulls for both communities in 1250 and 1253.[110] In these documents, the popes used the word *parochia* to mean a territorial unit of spiritual authority smaller than the diocese, coextensive with the monastic estate, and encompassing networks of local churches appropriated into the estate.[111] Their concern with proliferation of churches within the *parochiae* matches Bishop Lawrence's anticipation of 1217 regarding the monks of Lubiąż. These documents reflect, and anticipate, a steady rise in demand for spiritual care in the regions within which the monastery was established and endowed. Each of the communities presided over a small network of parishes under its patronage. Just how they exercised supervision over their parish networks is unclear. Conceivably, the monks performed spiritual

---

[106]*S.U.*, 1: no. 156–57 (1217), 113–14.

[107]Ibid., no. 157 (1217), 114: "quecumque ecclesie infra hos limites in posterum surrexerint sint filie matricis ecclesie, salvo in omnibus iure huius matricis ecclesie."

[108]Ibid., no. 75 (1201), 49.

[109]Ibid., no. 60–61 (1193), 37, 40.

[110]Ibid., 2: no. 397 (1250), 252, lines 26–28; 3: no. 89 (1253), 67, lines 42–44.

[111]For some reason, the popes were, on the face of the record, a bit less generous to the monks of Lubiąż; in their protective bulls for the community of 1216 and 1227, Innocent III and Gregory IX used the term 'parochia' in its usual meaning of the diocese of Wrocław, and did not either anticipate or record Bishop Lawrence's plans for turning that monastic estate into a small parish network. Ibid., 1: no. 148 (1216), 107; no. 279 (1227), 205.

care in the appropriated churches themselves, as they had done in other regions of Europe despite occasional canonical prohibitions to the contrary.[112]

Staffing these clusters of parishes with clergy must have been a continuous challenge, because the localities in which they were situated were among some of the most economically and demographically dynamic in Silesia. Evidence concerning the appropriated parishes situates the early Polish parish in a broad demographic, social, and economic context, and constitutes an important source of evidence about that context.[113] The number of parish churches in central Silesia increased steadily between the mid-twelfth and early thirteenth centuries. In 1201, the *parochia* of the canons regular of St. Vincent's included seven local churches.[114] Three of them were established between 1149 and 1201, that is, after the episcopate of Walter but before the end of the episcopate of Cyprian.[115] Thus, of the seven local churches

---

[112]Later evidence suggests that the canons regular of Wrocław controlled recruitment of their parish clergy rather than played that role themselves; more on this subject below.

[113]The following reconstructions are based on the following documents: *S.U.*, 1: no. 19 (1139–49), 15; no. 45 (1175), 28; no. 67 (1201), 48–49; no. 75 (1201), 49; no. 82 (1202), 54; no. 85 (1203), 59; no. 88 (1203), 61; no. 171 (1218), 123–26; 2: no. 397 (1250), 252; 3: no. 89 (1253), 67. Part of the impression of the rise in the number of local churches results from an improvement in the record; in particular, Bishop Cyprian's and Pope Innocent III's lists of churches in possession of the Wrocław canons regular, issued in 1201 and 1203, and the lists of the churches appropriated by the monks of Lubiąż compiled by Bishop Cyprian in 1201 and Bishop Lawrence in 1217, are more detailed than any previous references to local churches. The mention of a heretofore undocumented church in one of these surveys does not necessarily indicate anything about the time it was established. The specific inferences about the formation of new churches are drawn from internal evidence of these sources, as indicated in the footnotes below.

[114]*S.U.*, 1: no. 75 (1201), 48–49 (Innocent III); no. 85 (1203), 59 (Cyprian). Pope Innocent III's letter of 1201 for the canons of St. Vincent's notes "the church of St. Godard in Kostomłoty, St. Mary in Lusina, Sts. Blasius and Speratus in Oława, St. Peter in Toszek, St. James of Żuków, St. Margaret in Bytom, [and] St. Mary Magdalen in Kreszczenica." (p. 49). Please see Map 2.

[115]These include St. Godard's in Kostomłoty, St. Mary's in Lusina, and St. Mary Magdalen's in Kreszczenica. The inference of the time of their foundation is circumstantial. An early record of 1149 refers to "a market in Kostomłoty," but does not include that place in the list of churches granted to the canons; in 1201, Pope Innocent clearly indicated a presence of a local church there. The same early record includes Kreszczenica among the nineteen villages named at the end of the document of 1149–50, but does not mention a church. In 1203, Bishop Cyprian noted that he had granted that local church to the monastery and endowed it with a tithe. Sometime before 1149, the village of Lusina and its tithe revenue had been granted into the endowment of a church of St. Peter at Strzegom. That church had been consecrated by Bishop Walter. In 1203, Bishop Cyprian of Wrocław confirmed an earlier grant "of the church of St. Peter in Strzegom with all its appurtenances and with the village which is called Lusina" to a house of the Hospitallers near Wrocław, and added "the names of the villages whose tithes my predecessor of good memory, Walter, granted during the consecration of that church." The names of six places follow, starting with "Strzegom itself." Thus, the church of St. Mary's in Lusina had clearly been established between 1149 and 1201. Ibid., no. 75 (1201), 49; no. 85 (1203), 59; no. 88 (1203), 61. The documentation says nothing about the origins of the remaining four churches; thus, of course, they cannot be assumed to have been established prior to 1149.

Map 3. Parishes of Lubiąż, Ujazd, and Słup, 1202, 1203 and 1217 (*cura animarum*)

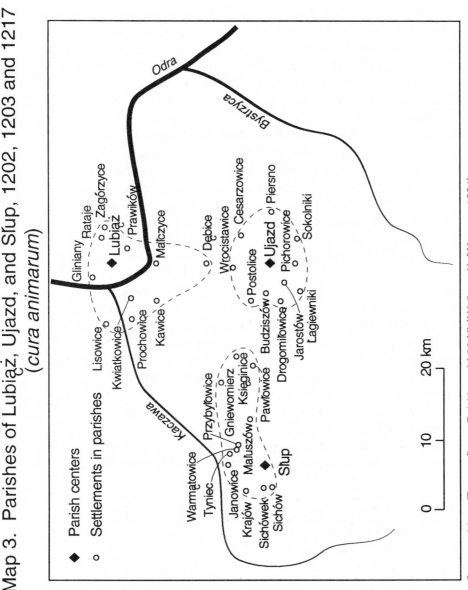

Source: *Mapa Topograficzna Polski*, no. M-33-XI (*Walbrzych*) (Warsaw, 1991).

possessed by the canons regular of St. Vincent's in 1201, at least three trace their origins to the second half of the preceding century. Of the local churches endowed with the *cura animarum* by Bishop Lawrence in 1217, two were probably established between 1175 and 1202, and one, the church of St. Mary's at Ujazd, was clearly established during the episcopate of Lawrence, that is after 1207.[116] Although these numbers are modest, they do suggest a brisk pace of expansion of new local churches in central Silesia, especially in conjunction with anticipation of the further expansion in their numbers and function.

The appropriated local churches that had parochial status at the time of the appropriation, or that acquired it as a result, were usually situated in areas of relatively intensive economic activity and demographic expansion. Of the three parish churches that acquired "cure of souls" in 1217 under patronage of the monks of Lubiąż, three were situated in areas of relatively intensive economic activity and population expansion. The parish church of St. John's was established within Lubiąż itself, "in the market."[117] Lubiąż and the church of St. John had been a nexus of lucrative activity for at least the preceding forty years. In 1175, Duke Bolesław the Tall gave the monks "Lubiąż and its appurtenances, that is, the church of St. John the Evangelist, the market with all uses, and the passage on the river with its district and everything in it."[118] The two churches of St. Mary's in Słup and in Ujazd were closely associated with demographic expansion. One was an offshoot of the other. The center of the older parish was Słup, while the center of the newer parish was Ujazd.

Between 1202 and 1207, the parish of church of St. Mary's in Słup was subdivided into two parishes under the calling of the same saint.[119] The older parish of St. Mary's continued to attract

---

[116]Ibid., no. 82 (1202), 54 (Bishop Cyprian); no. 156 (1217), 113 (Bishop Lawrence). Bishop Cyprian's list of local churches of the monks of Lubiąż that received tithes includes the churches of St. James's, St. John's, St. Mary's, and St. Peter's "of Wrocław"; Bishop Lawrence's list of parishes for the monks of Lubiąż includes the churches of St. John's "in the market" in Lubiąż, St. Mary's in Słup, and St. Mary's in Ujazd.

[117]Ibid., no. 156 (1217), 113.

[118]Ibid., no. 45 (1175), 28.

[119]Although in 1202 Bishop Cyprian recorded only one local church devoted to St. Mary in the Lubiąż estate, in 1217 Bishop Lawrence recorded two. One of these two churches was situated in Słup, the other in Ujazd. A comparison of the lists of place-names associated with both churches suggests that the area of settlement around Ujazd was relatively new. Except for the parish center of Ujazd itself, the places recorded in 1217 in the parish of "the church of St. Mary, the Virgin, in Ujazd," do not include any of the villages which had been recorded as sources of tithes for the church of St. Mary's recorded in 1202. It therefore seems that the parish of church of St. Mary's in Słup recorded in 1202 was during the subsequent fifteen years subdivided into two parishes under the calling of the same saint. The center of the older parish was Słup, while the center of the newer parish

settlement. The names of the localities recorded in the parish of
Słup strongly suggest that expansion was underway. Two localities recorded in 1202 were probably satellites of each other; they
were "Wołów and again (*item*) Wołów," and Parvum Malucz.[120]
In 1218, Bishop Lawrence repeated the reference to the tithes "of
Wołów and the other Wołów," and noted tithe "from Knejnice
near Parvum Malucz."[121] In 1217, he recorded "Sichów and the
other Sichów" in the same parish.[122] Two other villages, "Krajów
and Little Krajów" (*Kraiewo et Paruum Kraiewo*), were clearly a core
and a satellite village. Ujazd was an important locality throughout the first two decades of the thirteenth century. Before 1202, it
had belonged to Gniewomir, father of the ducal castellan named
Emmeram who endowed the Hospitallers with his church at
Strzegom.[123] Thereafter, it was an a magnet for settlement. In
1202, Bishop Cyprian simply referred to it as Ujazd, and placed it
near the end of the list of villages which owed tithes to the church
of St. Mary in Słup. In 1217, Bishop Lawrence referred to Ujazd as
a consisting of "the upper and the lower village" (*superior et inferior villa*), and listed it first in the list of villages which owed
tithe to its new parish church.[124]

The relatively dynamic localities included in the estate of the
monks of Lubiąż attracted German immigrants during this period. The documents record migration into the monastic estate by
Germans or by other settlers on terms modeled after the patterns
of German settlement between 1202 and 1218. In 1218, Bishop
Lawrence granted the monks "the right of tithe which had belonged to us in the forest [extending] up to Goldberg in the
neighborhood of Słup near [a settlement of] the Germans."[125]
They were to receive tithes from this region "whoever the estate
[to be established there] should belong to."[126] The forest specifically intended for clearing and lordship was situated near the

---

was Ujazd. In the 1218 document, Bishop Lawrence added that he had himself consecrated
the parish church at Ujazd. Among other tithes, he confirmed a grant of the tithe revenue
from an area of land "which had [formerly] belonged to the bishop's table . . . to the
church of St. Mary and of Sts. Martin and Cecilia in Ujazd, which we had consecrated."
Since Lawrence became bishop in 1202, the Ujazd parish church must have been consecrated between 1202 and 1217. Ibid., no. 82 (1202), 54; no. 156 (1217), 113; no. 171 (1218), 125.

[120]Ibid., no. 82 (1202), 54: "Wolowo, item Wolowo, Paruum Maluts."
[121]Ibid., no. 171 (1218), 125: "confirmamus decimas istarum villarum: Wolouo et alterius
Wolouo . . . decimam de Gneginiz iuxta parvum Maluzc."
[122]Ibid., no. 156 (1217), 113: "Sychouici et alii Sychouici."
[123]Ibid., no. 77 (1202), 50.
[124]Ibid., no. 156 (1217), 113: "ad ecclesiam sancte Marie virginis in Viazd: superior et
inferior villa."
[125]Ibid., no. 171 (1218), 125.
[126]Ibid.

expanding parish center of Słup, near the substantial German settlement of Goldberg, and near another German settlement that had no name in 1218, and thus must have been recent destination of German settlers.[127]

At the same time, the parish of Ujazd also served as a destination for German immigrants. Between 1202 and 1218, one of the villages included in the parish of Ujazd was reorganized as an estate held "according to German law." In his list of villages of 1202, Bishop Cyprian referred to "the village of Bartholomew"; in 1218, Bishop Lawrence called it "the village of Bartholomew, now called Schönwelt, with its entire district (*circuitus*)."[128] Before its grant to the monks, this estate had been a prebend of James, archdeacon of Wrocław. When the monks of Lubiąż received it in 1218, James received grain rents from another holding established "according to German law" in compensation. However, that other holding was only in the planning stage as of 1218. The level of grain rent it would produce was not clear, and the bishop fixed a range of compensations that James could expect in exchange for forgoing the tithe revenue from Schönwelt. Lawrence noted that in exchange for the tithe revenue at Schönwelt, James had[129]

accepted from the [monastic] church of Lubiąż [the revenue of] six [grain measures called] *maldratae* from the Germans of Oława. . . . If it should happen that less than six *maldratae* should accrue to this house [from this settlement of Germans], the house is obliged to fulfill the said James's prebend there and in that manner forever. And if more than six *maldratae* should accrue to this house [from this settlement of Germans], it should belong to the chapter of Wrocław.

This plan sheds some light on the process of German migration into the local society included in the estate of the monks of Lubiąż. German settlement in Oława had been underway before 1218; tithes from the settlers had been due to the monks of Lubiąż. Bishop Lawrence expected the level of tithe revenues from the German settlement to vary around six measures. If the level of anticipated immigration proved disappointing, the dio-

---

[127]Goldberg had been an important destination of German immigrants into Silesia since before 1211, and acquired formal town rights that year; Walter Kuhn, "Die Entstehung des mittelalterlichen schlesichen Kraftfeldes," in Walter Kuhn, *Beiträge zur schlesischen Siedlungsgeschichte* (Munich, 1971), 9–31 at 11–12; Josef Joachim Menzel, *Die schlesischen Lokationsurkunden des 13. Jahrhunderts* (Würzburg, 1977), pp. 123–25; Górecki, *Economy,*, 203–04, 244.
[128]Ibid., no. 74 (1202), 48 ("villa Bartolomei"); no. 171 (1218), 124 ("*villa Bartholomei que modo vocatur Sconiuelt, cum toto circuitu*").
[129]Ibid., no. 171 (1218), 124–25.

cese would subsidize tithe revenues of the archdeacon and the chapter. In this sense, the chapter of Wrocław underwrote, or guaranteed, that the monks would receive a particular level of revenue from a highly contingent level of anticipated settlement. The level of grain revenues promised the archdeacon from the anticipated German settlement was modest. Six *maldratae* of grain would be a level of revenue expected from six hides (*mansi*) of arable held "according to German law." This level of wealth in land and revenue is comparable to what a pioneering German settler might expect as compensation for recruiting, settling, and managing a group of other German settlers in Silesia.[130] The document does not state what proportion of the arable land of the German settlement at Oława was to be subjected to this tithe payment. Thus, the expected size of the planned German settlement cannot be assessed and its size was thus expected to be rather fluid. On another occasion there was some confusion about the exact place in which a settlement of Germans was currently situated. In a grant to another new monastery of 1210, Bishop Lawrence noted the settlement called "Goła with the Germans, who are said to hold [land] in Kietliny."[131] These plans suggest that during the early decades of the thirteenth century, German immigration into Silesia was a lucrative but possibly uncertain source of revenue.

German immigration led to expansion in the number of parish churches. In 1226, Bishop Lawrence gave the monks of Lubiąż tithe revenue from part of a region that was in the process of demographic expansion, German immigration, and multiplication of parish churches during the first three decades of the thirteenth century. The expanding area of settlement was situated about five kilometers to the west of Krosno, an important destination of German settlement in the same period.[132] In 1202, that area of settlement had a Polish place-name, Osiecznica. That year, Duke Henry gave the monks "the part of Osiecznica situated on this side of Sarbia," and added that Bishop Cyprian granted the tithe revenue from that portion of the locality.[133] Osiecznica must have been a rather sprawling locality; perhaps it was an expanding settlement. It was situated in an inhabited area; Henry "perambulated it with many neighbors" before

---

[130]Górecki, *Economy,*, 212–13, 215–6, 237–40.

[131]*S.U.*, 1: no. 122 (1210), 89: "Gola cum Teutonicis qui in Kydlinis dicuntur manere."

[132]For the expansion specifically of German settlement in this castellany, see Kuhn, "Kastellaneigrentzen," 13–25.

[133]*S.U.*, 1: no. 77 (1202), 50–51. Sarbia is today situated on the Odra about 15 km. west of Krosno; in 1202, part of that settlement may have been situated north of that river.

he gave it to the monks.[134] During the following decades Osiec-znica became a destination specifically of German settlement, which directly prompted the foundation of a new church in the locality. Bishop Lawrence noted in 1226 that "the village which was called Osiecznica . . . is now divided into two vil-lages, one of which the Germans call Mönchsdorf, the other Güntersberg."[135] He consecrated a church of St. Martin's in Mönchsdorf, "on a public road."[136] Once again, the new church was located in an economically important place, with relatively heavy traffic. Lawrence added that the location would enable it to perform the obligation of hospitality, an important step in its elevation to parish status.[137]

The foundation of the church at Mönchsdorf affected the finan-cial and spiritual interests of the parish clergy of Krosno. Lawrence endowed the new church at Mönchsdorf with tithe rev-enue from both new German settlements, "with consent of lord Siebracht, parish priest (plebanus) of St. Andrew's," who "used to receive tithe in the . . . territory."[138] St. Andrew's was the parish church of Krosno; in addition, Siebracht had been an archpriest (archipresbiter) there.[139] This latter term suggests that Siebracht enjoyed some kind of seniority over other clerics involved in ad-ministering spiritual care in the district of Krosno, and super-vised churches in the district of St. Andrew's of less than parochial status or of a more recent date. Indeed, before 1226 Sie-bracht had performed spiritual care for the expanding population of the former Osiecznica, but found that role increasingly diffi-cult, and took on other priests to help him. Lawrence noted that Siebracht had "provided cure of souls," in the expanding settle-ment, "but he found this dangerous, and he preferred to make a parish priest of Mönchsdorf a partner in the remuneration."[140] The initiative for procuring additional personnel thus came from Siebracht. Thereafter, he enjoyed a position of seniority over a new priest to be established in the new church in Mönchsdorf.

---

[134]Ibid.
[135]Ibid., no. 257–58 (1226), 187–89.
[136]Ibid.
[137]Ibid., no. 258 (1226), 189. For hospitality as one of the functions of parish churches, see Aubrun, La Paroisse, 52, 98–99.
[138]Ibid., no. 258 (1226), 189.
[139]Ibid. The term archpriest is rather rare in the Polish documents of the twelfth and thirteenth centuries. For the general meaning of the term archpriest, see J. M. Wallace-Hadrill, The Frankish Church (Oxford, 1983), 287; Aubrun, La Paroisse , 25–26, 49, 52; and in the Polish context, Szymański, "Biskupstwa," 227; Silnicki, Dzieje, 350–51.
[140]Ibid.

Siebracht's request and Lawrence's consent in 1226 trace out the division of spiritual responsibility among an older and a new church, and within a small hierarchy of parish priests. That hierarchy consisted of Siebracht, the new priest of St. Martin's, and another "parish priest (*plebanus*) of Krosno" named John.[141] Lawrence says nothing about John; perhaps he was Siebracht's subordinate in the performance of spiritual care within Krosno itself, as that settlement increased in size and importance. The relationship of the clerics of Krosno and Mönchsdorf explains the meaning and significance of archpriests in the context of population expansion. In 1226, Bishop Lawrence used the term to refer to a cleric with parochial responsibilities over a substantial area of expanding settlement, who enjoyed or required assistance from other parish priests in their performance.[142] In subsequent years, Siebracht did not retire from his spiritual responsibilities; he was still parish priest of St. Andrew's in 1231.[143] Thus, neither the hierarchy not Siebracht's presence in it were transient.

The monks of Lubiąż sought to establish parishes in other regions of the duchy that were undergoing demographic and economic expansion. Between 1214 and 1226, Bishop Lawrence issued several documents recording the monastic initiatives in a region situated about fifty kilometers to the south of Wrocław, between two tributaries of the Odra called the Osobłoga and the Stradunia.[144] That region had a fairly long history of demographic expansion. Around the turn of the twelfth and thirteenth centuries, two lords had encouraged settlement in this region; the first was Lawrence's predecessor, Bishop Jarosław of Wrocław, the second was Duke Casimir of Opole. Between 1212 and 1214, Lawrence noted that Jarosław had granted tithe revenue "from [his estate called] Jarosław," consisting of seven localities with Polish place-names, and from "any villages established in the future between the boundaries of Głogówek and Jarosław, now called Kazimierz up to the rivers Stradunia and Osobłoga, where these two together flow into the [river] Odra, with what[ever] increase should be there in the future."[145] The Polish place-names

---

[141]Ibid.

[142]Ibid., 1: no. 258 (1226), 189.

[143]Ibid., 2: no. 2 (1231), 1, line 45.

[144]*S.U.*, 1: no. 143 (1212–14), 101–02; no. 171 (1218), 125; no. 182 (1218), 136; no. 231 (1223), 168–69; no. 271 (1226). For a treatment of settlement in this region, characteristically with stress solely on Germans, see Walter Kuhn, *Siedlungsgeschichte Oberschlesiens* (Würzburg, 1954), 51–52.

[145]*S.U.*, 1: no. 143 (1212–14), 101–02.

suggest that new clearings were to take place within or near a previously inhabited area.

Settlement between the two rivers increased over subsequent years. The result was conflict over possession of tithe from the new clearing in the Osobłoga-Stradunia-Odra fork between the monks of Lubiąż and other tithe possessors. In 1218, Bishop Lawrence observed that one settlement, Łowkowice, had expanded across the Osobłoga into the territory. The claimant against the monks was a possessor of tithe revenue from the older portion of Łowkowice, on the outer side of the river. Lawrence did not identify the claimant, merely noted that "the other party believed" that the tithe obligation of the newly cleared portion of the village "should follow the [older] other part of the village beyond the Osobłoga."[146] He dismissed the claim with a reminder that "the right to gather tithe between the said rivers has belonged to the [monks] of Lubiąż since long ago," and for good measure added that "the right to gather tithe from one village often belongs to many." [147] The conflict suggests vigorous competition for tithe revenues from regions undergoing demographic expansion. Lawrence's selection of rationale for rightful possession of tithes from newly cleared arable suggest that this type of conflict was recurrent, and that the Polish clergy of the turn of the twelfth and thirteenth centuries relied on a variety of formal legal norms to resolve it.

Indeed, the monks of Lubiąż acquired noval tithes in other regions of expanding settlement in Silesia, and faced conflict in the process. One such region was the vicinity of Legnica. In 1175, Duke Bolesław the Tall and Bishop Żyrosław of Wrocław jointly promised the monks of Lubiąż tithes "from new villages now existing in the district of Legnica, and from [villages] to be established there for all time."[148] The tithe revenue forgone in 1175 must have been substantial, because Bishop Jarosław, Żyrosław's successor between 1198 and 1201, had "objected to the gift of [tithes from] the new fields (donatio novalium) made by lord Żyrosław the bishop to the monastery of Lubiąż."[149] The results of Jarosław's objections are unknown. Nevertheless, Jarosław

---

[146]Ibid.

[147]Ibid., no. 182 (1218), 136.

[148]Ibid., no. 45 (1175), 28.

[149]M.P.H., 3: 547. This passage is excerpted from a list of the bishops of Wrocław, inserted into a fifteenth-century chronicle, Chronica Principum Polonie, edited by Zygmunt Węclewski in M.P.H., 3: 423–578, at 544–78 (chap. 37, De insitutione ecclesie Wratislaviensis). This compilation is based on earlier documents; see Heck, "Silesian Historiography," 65, n. 9.

was remembered specifically for raising this issue, suggesting that the conflict was of some importance. Perhaps one party to the conflict was the parish church of St. Mary's in Legnica.[150]

A generation later, Duke Henry recorded in 1211 his gift of "tithe in [the district of] Legnica from the entire field of Sławno" to the Lubiąż community, and Bishop Lawrence confirmed tithes "from Sławno near Legnica" in 1218.[151] "Whether the arable there belongs to us, to our sons and successors, or to anyone else, the tithe there shall be paid in full to the monastery."[152] Sławno was essentially a unit of arable, to be put to unspecified future use. Actual possession and presumably exploitation of this unit of arable were expected to vary with time, but the monks' possession of tithe from it was to survive any such variation.

In yet another region, failure by the monks of Lubiąż to clarify their rights to noval tithes led to conflict with the bishops of Wrocław, who claimed the right to collect these tithes in the absence of an explicit grant of that right to the monks. The difficulty originated sometime between 1170 and 1198, when Bishop Żyrosław gave the monks the tithe revenues from the village of Dziewin. Bishop Lawrence recalled in 1215 that Żyrosław, "had fully granted the tithes of his village called Dziewin to the monastery of Lubiąż," and that the monks "held [the tithes] by quiet right in continuous possession."[153] The legal tranquillity lasted until a sharp expansion of settlement in the region sometime before 1198[154]:

After a passage of time, the peasants (*agricolae*) of the nearest village called Kliszów, situated across the adjacent bank of the river [dividing the two villages], began to clear the forest in order to expand new lands (*ad extendenda novalia*); and from the other side the settlers (*coloni*) of the other village, which is called Dziewin, undertook to expand their new lands by extirpating [the forest] (*extirpando novalia sua extenderunt*). So a serious quarrel arose among the settlers of each village during the collection of tithes.

Why did claims to tithes lead to conflict among the two peasant groups? I would guess that each group was expanding towards the river that separated the two villages, that each considered the

---

[150]Noted by Duke Henry in his charter of 1202 or 1203 for the nuns of Trzebnica. *S.U.*,1: no. 83 (1202–03), 57.
[151]*S.U.*, 1: no. 123 (1211), 90; no. 171 (1218), 125.
[152]Ibid., no. 123 (1211), 90.
[153]Ibid., no. 144 (1215), 103.
[154]Ibid.

area across the river as a territory open to its further expansion, and that the ecclesiastics who claimed tithes from each group— the monks in the case of the settlers at Dziewin, and the bishop in the case of the settlers at Kliszów—asserted noval tithes over the area of the river and its banks into which both groups of peasants had expanded over the preceding two or three decades. This could have resulted in a claim for two noval tithes for each group from the territory affected, and prompted each group to insist that the other group cease its expansion in the direction in which they had been expanding. Bishop Żyrosław arranged a compromise which seems to bear out that that was the nature of the conflict among the two groups of peasants; he assigned to each ecclesiastical institution the noval tithes from the village on its own side of the river.[155]

Sometime between 1214 and 1226, the monks of Lubiąż undertook to establish a parish church in one of the expanding regions in which they acquired noval tithes. In 1223, "on petition of . . . lord Gunther, abbot of Lubiąż," Bishop Lawrence "established the boundaries of the church of St. Mary's in Kazimierz between the rivers Osobłoga and Stradunia, with all the villages established or to be established there."[156] However, on this occasion, he explicitly denied the monks tithe revenues from a particular locality within the river region, which, as he put it, "belonged to" an older place of settlement, and from thirteen specified localities situated "beyond the Stradunia."[157] He clearly feared a recurrence of the type of conflict he had had resolved four years earlier respecting Łowkowice. He also implied that the monks were formulating plans to reach outside the river region and acquire tithe revenues of neighboring possessors, and drew a firm line at the river boundary. This provision represents a culminating point of assigning tithe revenues from the region and the immediately surrounding areas in the face of settlement expansion and competition for possession of tithe revenues.

Struggles over noval tithes suggest that at least parts of Silesia experienced pressure on land and intensification of agriculture by the early decades of the thirteenth century. Records of one parish church directly reflect intensification of agriculture. In a document contemporary with his grant of "cure of souls" to the monks of Lubiąż but for once not intended for their benefit, Bishop Lawrence sketched out the history of two churches situ-

---

[155]Ibid., 102–03.
[156]Ibid., no. 171 (1218), 125.
[157]Ibid.

ated in the castellany of Wleń. The aim of the document was to furnish the more recently established church with tithe revenue. This was a church of St. Mary's in Bystrzyca; Lawrence did not specify its status, but did note that the tithe revenue assigned to it had formerly been possessed by the church of St. Mary's in Wleń and its parish priest (*parochianus*) named Henry the Bavarian.[158] The parish priest of St. Mary's in Wleń had possessed that tithe ever since the consecration of that church by Bishop Walter around the mid-twelfth century.[159] Between 1202 and 1217, Duke Henry and his wife, Duchess Hedwig, arranged for the tithe from Bystrzyca to be paid in grain, not squirrel skins; and in 1217, the bishop granted that tithe revenue to the new church of St. Mary's in Bystrzyca.[160] In addition, the new church was endowed with a fairly substantial estate. The church "shall also have," Lawrence provided, "a mill with two taverns in Bystrzyca. In addition an estate [consisting of] four oxen and a horse, and winter and summer seed."[161] The shift in the tithe obligations to grain, the grant of a grain-producing farmstead, and the grant of a mill suggest a shift towards more intensive agriculture in the locality of Bystrzyca between the turn of the century and 1217.[162] The grant of taverns must have been intended as a source of coin revenue.[163]

The records of local churches appropriated or established by the major Silesian monasteries in central Silesia during the twelfth and earlier thirteenth centuries give the first approximation of the network of parochial care around the turn of the thirteenth century. That network was comparatively diffuse and dispersed. At its outermost geographic limit, the network of local churches appropriated by the canons of St. Mary's and St.

---

[158]*S.U.*, 1: no. 164 (1217), 117.

[159]Ibid.

[160]Ibid.

[161]Ibid.

[162]Grants of farmsteads reckoned in four-ox units, with or without horses, recur in the Polish estate foundations of the early twelfth century. The most important use of this unit is the large survey of the estate of the nuns of Trzebnica, compiled around 1204; in addition, two farmsteads thus designated were granted to the Wrocław houses of St. Mary's and St. Vincent's in 1204. I have hypothesized that the unit of four oxen plus a horse is a trace of the diffusion of the mouldboard plow on the major monastic estates in Silesia; see my discussion in *Economy*, 49–50, indebted to John Langdon, *Horses, Oxen, and Technological Innovation: The Use of Draught Animals in English Farming from 1066–1500* (Cambridge, 1986), 34, 62–74, 118–27, 296.

[163]On the crucial role of taverns in the earlier medieval Polish economy, see Irena Cieśla, "Taberna wczesnośredniowieczna na ziemiach polskich" [The early medieval tavern in Poland], *Studia Wczesnośredniowieczne*, 4 (1958): 159–225; Irena Rabęcka-Brykczyńska and Franciszek Sławski, "Karczma" [The tavern], *Słownik Starożytności Słowiańskich*, 2 (1964): 373–75; Irena Rabęcka, "The Early Medieval Tavern in Poland," *Ergon*, 3 (1962): 372–75; Górecki, *Economy*, 51–55, 63–64.

Vincent's spanned the entire duchy of Silesia. It extended for about 200 kilometers, from Bytom in the northwest of the duchy to Toszek in the southeast. Within these outer limits, the churches appropriated by the canons were distributed unevenly. Most were situated in the relatively well-documented region of central Silesia, and formed part of a relatively close network of parishes there. Of the nine local churches recorded in the documents of 1201 and 1203, eight were situated within on average a bit over twenty kilometers of one another. Of these eight, four were situated within the core areas of settlement in Legnica and Wrocław, and three within the relatively well-documented river system of the middle Odra and the Bystrzyca. Of those three, the two at Lusina and Kostomłoty were situated about ten kilometers apart.

Similarly, the three parish churches with "cure of souls" situated at Słup, Ujazd, and Lubiąż, and appropriated by the monks of Lubiąż, were situated between seven and ten kilometers from each other within the same region. Overall, this region included eleven local churches, of which the three located at Słup, Ujazd, and Lubiąż are explicitly recorded as possessing "cure of souls." The average distance between all local churches in the region appropriated by the three monastic communities of Wrocław and Lubiąż was just over twenty kilometers. This parish network was dispersed by earlier medieval standards. The documented distances between parish centers fall on the large end of the range of distances between rural parish churches and the settlements they serviced in some of the more carefully studied regions of Europe between the ninth and twelfth centuries.[164]

Parishes tended to be centered in the more demographically and economically dynamic localities within the sub-region. The centers were surrounded with a substantial number of outlying villages. The areas of settlement associated with these local churches are recorded in Bishop Lawrence's lists of villages over which the parish churches at Lubiąż, Słup, and Ujazd were to possess "cure of souls," as of 1217. Not all of the places he listed can be identified, but a fairly clear pattern is formed by those

---

[164]For information about distances between parish centers, sizes of parishes in terms of surface areas, and occasionally population sizes in various regions of earlier medieval Europe, see, among others: Wendy Davies, *Small Worlds: The Village Community in Early Medieval Brittany* (Berkeley–Los Angeles, 1988), 64–66, and n. 11; Duby, *Société*, 230–31; Gabriel Fournier, "Le mise en place du cadre paroissial et l'évolution du peuplement," *Settimane di studio del Centro italiano di studi sull'alto medioevo*, 28 (Spoleto, 1982): 495–563, especially the case studies cited at 544–51; H. C. Darby, *Domesday England* (Cambridge, 1977), 52–56; Coste, "L'institution paroissiale," 311–17, and the cited literature; Burns, *Crusader Kingdom*, 1: 78–87; Łowmiański, *Religia*, 315–16.

places that can be. Each of the local churches was to possess "cure of souls" over a group of localities situated between two and thirteen kilometers away. All three parishes included some proportion of settlements situated within five kilometers of the center. Some of these settlements were considerably closer, and must have been outliers of the parish centers with distinct place-names. Thus, the distances from the parish centers to the settlements varied widely within the individual parishes and from one parish to another.

The least dispersed of the three parishes appropriated by the Lubiąż monks was at Ujazd; nevertheless, its territory was still large. The ten villages that were included in it and that can be identified on the map were all situated within a radius of six kilometers of Ujazd itself. Thus, the territory of the parish spanned over 100 square kilometers. The distances between the central settlement of Słup and the other villages included within that parish varied widely. Eight of these settlements were situated within six kilometers of Słup; this was the core region of the parish, more densely settled than the Ujazd parish. However, three other villages were situated relatively far, between twelve and fourteen kilometers to the north and northeast of Słup. This parish was therefore scattered at the periphery. Finally, the parish centered on the church of St. John in the market place of Lubiąż included villages within a rather more uniform range of distances from one another. All but one of the identifiable villages of that parish were situated within about eight kilometers of the parish center; the sole exception was one about fifteen kilometers to the south of Lubiąż. It was thus another territorially large parish, slightly larger than the parish of Ujazd. The parishes, though rather territorially large, were sharply articulated local hierarchies of settlement, economic activity, and cult.

The number of inhabitants of each region serviced by a local church at the outset of the thirteenth century can tentatively be reconstructed for only one locality, namely the region centered on Trzebnica. Duke Henry's grants contain an exceptionally good record of places and persons situated within the radius of about five kilometers of the village of Trzebnica and the local church of St. Peter in that village. The grants mention fourteen named localities within this radius; in addition, the grants refer to another eight named localities that were not included within the estate.[165]

---

[165]Górecki,"Economy, Society, and Lordship," 188–89, 238–86; Górecki; *Economy,* 23–26.

The entire area of settlement corresponds to the hierarchy of economy, demography, and cult which Bishop Lawrence integrated into parishes in 1217. Thus, the central place in which the local church was situated was economically and demographically the most active place within the region. It was the local center of exchange and specialized production, which Duke Henry the Bearded channeled into a new exempted market place between 1202 and 1208.[166] A substantial proportion of the listed inhabitants were intensively specialized peasants who carried the status of "guests"; they were evidently recent immigrants, and were subjected to relatively heavy agricultural rent obligations to the nuns.[167] This settlement was the largest included in the nuns' estate; the record notes 43 male names of settlers.[168] Other settlements were smaller, of uneven size, and inhabited by a smaller proportion of "guests," or none at all. Altogether, at least well over a thousand persons must have lived in the villages included in the nuns' estate in 1204 within the five kilometer radius of Trzebnica. Villages situated in the same locality but not included in the estate must have increased that number by a substantial margin. Altogether, the network of the individual settlements was fairly tight, and the total level of population within that network comparable to that of a parish of a moderate size in several other regions of medieval Europe.[169]

---

[166]Górecki, *Economy*, 51–55.
[167]Ibid., 25, 78–80.
[168]Ibid., 24.
[169]Coste, "L'institution paroissiale," 311–17.

2. SECULAR AND ECCLESIASTICAL CONTROL OVER PARISH CHURCHES

Local church clergy: performance, obedience, supervision, control

The actor curiously missing from the evidence of the arising structure of spiritual care is the cleric who performed it. Local clerics largely disappeared from the record even more fully than the churches they staffed until the early thirteenth century, when Pope Innocent III returned to the old theme of inadequacy of the Polish clergy with a vengeance. Two of the pope's seven short letters of 1207 are addressed to Polish clerics. One is addressed generally to all beneficed clerics "in Poland"; the other is addressed to "the chaplains of the duke and other nobles of Poland."[170] Both documents attempt to strengthen the internal organization of the Polish clergy, and to ensure the obedience of all clerics to their superiors and to the archbishop of Gniezno through a system of supervision and visitation by archdeacons. Bishops and legates returned to these concerns in the reform councils and statutes of the thirteenth century. The resulting evidence documents the functions and effectiveness of parish clergy and the relationship between secular power and parish churches in the archdiocese of Gniezno.

In one of his letters of 1207, Pope Innocent chastised the "chaplains" of Polish "dukes and nobles" for placing loyalty and service to their secular patrons above loyalty and service to bishops and abbots, and described the resulting harm[171]:

Although you serve secular lords, it does not become you to withhold due reverence and honor from ecclesiastical prelates. Thus by authority

---

[170]Ibid., no. 103–04 (1207), 74; the latter phrase is "ducis et aliorum nobilium Polonie capellanis."

[171]Ibid., no. 103 (1207), 74: "Cum ex eo quod secularibus dominis deservitis prelatis ecclesiasticis debitam subtrahere vos non deceat reverentiam et honorem, presentium vobis auctoritate mandamus et districte precipimus quatenus archidiaconos vestros, cum parrochiam visitando ad loca vestra pervenerint, honeste recipere studeatis et procurationem eis debitam exhibentes cathedratica que debentur archiepiscopo vel episcopis cum integritate debita persolvatis."

of the present [letter] we mandate and strictly command you that when your archdeacons arrive in your prebends (*loca*) in the course of visiting a parish, you shall attempt to receive them honorably, and you shall furnish them with a visitation payment (*cathedraticum*) due to the archbishop or bishops in the entirety.

The most conservative reading of this passage is that a substantial portion of the Polish clergy was engaged in "service" to "secular lords" as their "chaplains," and that the "secular lords" included the dukes and "nobles." The pope did not question the validity of that pattern of "service" and loyalty, but demanded that it be reconciled with "reverence and honor" due to bishops. He did not explain the functions the "chaplains" played for their patrons; he merely asserted that such functions were beyond effective control of the Polish bishops. Nor did he explain who the "nobles" were, but his terminology and identification of actors match Gallus's image of founders of local churches of a century earlier.

Innocent sought to strengthen a system of parochial visitation by archdeacons, and thus bring the archdiocese of Gniezno into conformity with the patterns of episcopal control of local churches and clergy that had been emerging in Western Europe for several centuries.[172] In the process, he illustrated some of the features and obstacles to this type of control specific to the Polish duchies. Rather cryptically, he noted that the "chaplains" were based within their own *loca*. What were they? Since in the absence of lay interference these *loca* would have been archdeacons' destinations during visitations, and places where archdeacons were entitled to hospitality, the *loca* were probably churches endowed with prebends or with other sources of revenue.[173] Each *parochia* contained several such places. The pope mandated the offending clerics to make each *locus* within the *parochia* available for visits by archdeacons, and to facilitate the visits with the *cathedraticum*, a specialized payment for that purpose.[174]

Innocent's use of the term *parochia* is a bit opaque. The only clear features of his *parochiae* is that they were destinations for vis-

---

[172]Wallace-Hadrill, *Frankish Church*, 286–88; Morris, *Papal Monarchy*, 222–23, 533–35; Aubrun, *La Paroisse*, 35–36, 48–49, 85–87, 119–22.

[173]Ordinarily, as used in the Polish documents, *locus* refers to a church, specifically the particular church which is the subject of the document. Monastic churches are frequently referred to with that term. It is also, of course, used in the more general sense of "place," or in both meanings at once to designate the locality in which a church is present or planned. The same meanings occur in general medieval usage, but *locus* may also mean the prebend used to support a particular church or cleric. See Niermeyer, 619–20, s.v. *locus*.

[174]Niermeyer, 158, s.v. *cathedraticum*.

itations of archdeacons, and that they consisted of networks of *loca*. Since archdeacons were episcopal agents, Innocent must have used the term *parochia* to mean a diocese or its subdivision, containing either several churches or prebends supporting groups of "chaplains." Thus, *parochia* may have meant a transitional stage between a diocese and a parish, if not indeed the parish.[175] Innocent's usage of 1207 partly corresponds to that of his immediate predecessor Celestine III, who meant by *parochia* the local churches under spiritual authority of a single monastic community. Although Innocent did not unequivocally use the term to mean a local church with the authority to administer sacraments, his usage is another example of its increasingly local meaning in the archdiocese of Gniezno at the turn of the twelfth and thirteenth centuries.

Innocent's glimpse into the local structure of the archdiocese of Gniezno is almost teasingly incomplete. Quite apart from the terminological difficulties, the normative scope of the document is not clear. Is the letter a blueprint for future territorial organization of episcopal control over localities? Or was Innocent assuming an existing network of *parochiae* and *loca*, to which archdeacons sought access but were frustrated by lay power? In other words, how much of the document was normative? Since Innocent framed the actual grievance in terms of access by archdeacons to actual administrative units, I would guess that the *parochiae* were actually in place in 1207.

In the subsequent decades, Polish bishops and papal legates explored the problems Innocent touched on in detail. They repeatedly focused on visitations by bishops and archdeacons, supervision and comportment of parish clergy, and the relationship between parish clergy and churches and secular power.[176] "We especially instruct all the archdeacons," noted Archbishop Pełka in the reform synod of 1233, "to carry out their office diligently by visiting churches and priests in person and not through others, unless they are detained by a just and adequate hindrance."[177] Beside failing to carry out visitations, archdeacons often avoided their responsibility altogether by entrusting visitations to other clerics; then they collected visitation payments from the parish priests whom they ought to have visited in

---

[175]This is in any event the earliest documented use of the term 'parochia' for an administrative district smaller than a diocese.

[176]For the functions of the archdeacons in medieval Poland, including visitation, see Tadeusz Silnicki, *Organizacja archidiakonatu w Polsce* [Organization of the archdeaconate in Poland] (Lwów, 1927); idem, *Dzieje*, 346–55; Szymański, "Biskupstwa," 220–30.

[177]*S.U.*, 2: no. 34 (1233), 21, lines 24–26.

person. "We also prohibit this," thundered Pełka, "that no one among them dare to exact anything from the priests as payment for visitation, and claim that is it owed by reason of visitation, when he did not carry out the visitation."[178] Fifteen years later, Legate James of Liège instructed the Polish bishops to "admonish your archdeacons . . . to visit churches in person."[179] He repeated Pełka's provision by stipulating that "archdeacons who do not visit . . . shall henceforth accept or demand no money for their cares;but shall have and demand [payment for] their care only when they visit the church in person."[180] He also fixed the level of payment the archdeacons could demand from the parish priest in that case.[181]

The implementation of these norms in practice is difficult to gauge; however, in one respect they were demonstrably not effective, and called for revision. Archdeacons continued to delegate their responsibility to other clerics, forcing Legate Guido to make the best of the situation in 1267. Like Pełka and James before him, he began by exhorting Polish bishops "to make good the archdeacons' negligence in the visitations of clerics, regardless of any custom," but then seriously modified Pełka's and James's view of what constituted performance of that obligation.[182] "No one shall receive money for a visit to be performed or for care," he wrote, "but when visitation is carried out by him [i.e., the archdeacon] or a worthy vicar, he [i.e., the vicar] shall be content with the cost of necessities of the administration, and the archdeacons themselves" shall receive from the parish priest the remuneration spelled out by James nineteen years earlier.[183] Guido limited the remuneration to the "necessities" of the visiting cleric, and to that extent was more restrictive than Pełka and James. On the other hand, he allowed the archdeacons to appoint vicars to perform visitations and receive remuneration for the vicars' work. Thus, he accommodated the previous practices, subject to conditions.

Who exactly were the local clerics over whom the archdeacons were exhorted to exercise control? In 1207, Innocent III said nothing specific about the "chaplains" to whom he hoped to enhance their access; later prelates clearly assumed that the *parochiae* of the turn of the century were filled by priests who staffed a network of

---

[178]Ibid., no. 34 (1233), 21, lines 26–28.
[179]Ibid., no. 346 (1248), 212, lines 41, 44.
[180]Ibid., no. 346 (1248), 212, lines 39, 42–44.
[181]Ibid., lines 44–45.
[182]Ibid., 4: no. 5 (1267), 8, lines 19–21.
[183]Ibid., lines 21–24.

parish churches. Like the archdeacons who were to visit and supervise them, the priests busily shirked their responsibilities in several ways. "According to a constitution of the [Fourth] Lateran Council," noted Archbishop Pełka in 1233,[184]

everyone shall personally serve in the parish church he holds, and shall reside in the [good] order required by the cure of that church. No one from among them may establish a vicar without our special license. All vicars of parish churches shall be established either by our special license and knowledge, or [by special license and knowledge] of our archdeacons, to whom examination of such persons belongs. Nor shall they be removed unless by a just cause, demonstrated to us or our archdeacons. Nor may a vicar himself establish a vicar in his function.

Of the very wide range of concerns addressed at the universal Church by the ecumenical council in 1215, the subject most relevant to the province of Gniezno during the subsequent decades was avoidance of pastoral responsibility by archdeacons and parish priests. It seems that at all rungs on the ladder clergy formally involved in the administration of spiritual care routinely sought to avoid their responsibilities. In 1233, Archbishop Pełka tried to bring the offending priests under supervision by archdeacons who, as he knew, sought to divest themselves of their own responsibilities through appointing vicars of their own. He confronted the irony by entrusting the supervisory function specifically to his own archdeacons, presumably a different cadre from the archdeacons of his suffragans. He provided a formal, inquisitorial procedure by which the entire supervisory personnel examined the qualifications of the vicars. Finally, he addressed the questions of the position of the licitly appointed vicars towards the rectors who appointed them by offering them protection from removal. In turn, he prohibited them from appointing their own vicars.

Juggling the realities of clerical supervision and avoidance occupied the Polish bishops well into the century. In his statutes issued between 1248 and 1257, Bishop Thomas spelled out a fairly elaborate mechanism to attempt to compel all priests to attend an annual synod. "From now on," he provided,[185]

everyone shall convene at the episcopal synod to be celebrated on the feast of St. Luke; and whoever does not excuse himself within fifteen

---

[184]Ibid., 22, line 14–23, line 4.
[185]Ibid., 126, lines 11–15.

days from the time of the synod, or provide satisfaction of three silver marks within the said time, shall be suspended by the action of law (*ipso iure*), and the archpriests shall raise accusations against the absent priests and give [the accusation] in writing to the archdeacon before they recede from the synod once a year, under the aforesaid penalty.

Thomas, again, engaged several categories of clergy who were or ought to have been active in the administration of spiritual care in an elaborate scheme of internal supervision. On this occasion, Thomas recruited into the sanction mechanism yet another intermediary between the bishop and the problematic parish priests, the archpriest. The canon clearly presumes that parish priests were a standard feature of the ecclesiastical life of the diocese and that they routinely avoided yet another obligation, namely, to attend the annual synod. The archpriest's effectiveness as a formal accuser of his underlings cannot be assessed, because that elusive figure once again lapses into its usual obscurity. Thomas himself recognized the limits of compulsion that could be brought to bear on recalcitrant priests by allowing excused absences and payments in lieu of attendance, subject to formal qualifications.

Bishops and legates sought to engage archdeacons and parish priests in enforcement of sentences of excommunication and in the promulgation of their own statutes. Legate James mandated in 1248 that archiepiscopal sentences of excommunication "shall be publicly announced in the cathedral church and in other churches of the city and diocese every Sunday, with festive candles lit, and with bells ringing."[186] James did not impose this obligation on specific clerics, but about nine years later Bishop Thomas explicitly placed it on parish priests. "Every Sunday at the time of the mass . . . , all parish priests shall excommunicate those whom the lord archbishop has excommunicated, with bells ringing and candles extinguished."[187] By 1267, Guido mandated use of the same institutional network to promulgate the statutes of the Wrocław council over which he presided:[188]

We wish and direct on pain of excommunication that the lord archbishop of Gniezno and his suffragans cause these constitutions of ours . . . to be recited and most closely observed in the episcopal synods and provincial council every year; and cause those [matters] that touch laymen to be made public through the parish churches of their diocesan [bishops].

---

[186]Ibid., 2: no. 346 (1248), 207, lines 10–12.
[187]Ibid., 3: no. 182 (1248–57), 126, lines 1–3.
[188]Ibid., 4: no. 5 (1267), 9, lines 1–5.

All these provisions and strategies of control are regional counterparts of the centralization of ecclesiastical authority throughout Europe, at the provincial and ecumenical levels. However, they are quite distinctive in their emphasis and detail. Throughout the first half of the thirteenth century, ecclesiastical reformers active in or concerned about the archdiocese of Gniezno routinely focused on close control over parish clergy by the regional hierarchy. In so doing, the refined one area of Innocent III's concerns about this province antedating the Fourth Lateran Council. The provisions of their legislation clearly assume, and reflect, the existence of a highly defined network of parishes and parish priests that was at least potentially capable of acting for several purposes.

One of these purposes was defense of local ecclesiastical institutions against secular power. The bishops and legates active between 1233 and 1267 recurrently addressed several problems of control by lay persons over churches, clerics, benefices, tithe revenues, and other ecclesiastical interests. These concerns hark back to Pope Innocent III's demands for clerical loyalty to ecclesiastical superiors of 1207, and indeed farther back to Gallus's twelfth-century image of secular "nobles" as creators of local churches and to the slightly later glimpses of its meaning. The basic theme of violence against churches, cemeteries, and clerics recurs in the conciliar documents. As in the case of other partial and authoritative complaints, it is difficult to assess the degree of the alleged damage; but the kind of damage alleged, the definitions of culpable parties, and the details of the planned excommunication are quite informative. The bishops' and prelates' exasperated descriptions of these grievances, and the remedies they fashioned, shed additional light on the function of parish churches in Poland within the half-century after Innocent first pushed the Polish clergy towards reform of that web of difficulties.

Archbishop Pełka devoted a substantial chapter of his canons of 1233 to this subject. He noted with regret that although "violators of churches and cemeteries" ought to be punished, "the magnates of the land are deterred neither by fear of God nor by honor of the churches."[189] In response, he devised an elaborate mechanism for at least attempting to control their behavior. He mandated the bishops to place excommunication and interdict on several parties. "Above all," they were to punish "the leader of

---

[189]Ibid., 2: no. 34 (1233), 21, lines 39–41.

the army (*princeps exercitus*) because of whom [the damages] were done."[190] Realizing that commanders of substantial military groups were likely to be indifferent to this type of sanction, Pełka widened the net of culpable parties to include more plausible subjects of excommunication. "In the event that none of the leaders is present in person, the punishment shall be inflicted especially on those who are the most important in the army (*principales in exercitu*)."[191] Elsewhere, he descended a bit farther down the ranks of potential offenders, and mandated excommunication of "whoever violates a church or cemetery, or whoever is among the more important leaders of this army (*de principalioribus illius exercitu*)."[192] All the sentences of excommunication were to last until the excommunicates performed adequate satisfaction for the damages to the churches, which, in view of his rather frantic search for culpable soldiers to excommunicate, Pełka clearly expected to take some time.[193]

In his search for hierarchies of associates in crime, the archbishop may have been adopting a strategy by which ecclesiastics throughout Europe sought to overcome limits on authoritative control of lay populations during the first half the early thirteenth century. Theories of vicarious culpability and agency in crime were developed in other regions of Europe specifically to combat dissent.[194] Legate James, who later threatened to excommunicate "all burners and destroyers of churches and spoilers of cemeteries," as well as "those by whose counsel, aid, or mandate these things should be done in the future,"[195] also mandated introduction of elements of the contemporary inquisitorial procedure and penalties into the archdiocese of Gniezno.[196] Although the effects of these plans are entirely inaccessible, for present purposes Pełka's and James's documents suggest the significance of contemporary innovations in theories of liability and judicial procedure in a context very different from religious dissent, but no less urgent in this particular province.

Aside from broadening the roster of culpable parties, the prelates repeatedly threatened interdict against churches in posses-

---

[190]Ibid., 2: no. 34 (1233), 21, lines 43–44.
[191]Ibid., 21, line 4423, line 1.
[192]Ibid., 23, lines 3–4.
[193]Ibid., lines 2–3, 4–5, 8–9.
[194]Henry Charles Lea, *A History of the Inquisition of the Middle Ages* (New York, 1888, repr. 1955), 1: 321–22, 505–06, 507; an excellent selection of translated documents that address vicarious responsibility is Edward Peters (ed.), *Heresy and Authority in Medieval Europe* (Philadelphia, 1977), 169, 172–73, 175–76, 197, 209, 211.
[195]*S.U.*, 2: no. 346 (1248), 212, lines 13–15.
[196]Ibid., 206, lines 5, 9–15, 33–38.

sion of the laity. Archbishop Pełka did not rest with the somewhat helpless strategy of excluding the intractable culprits from the sacraments and waiting; he added that "all the churches in which they have right of patronage shall be suspended, and no divine offices shall be celebrated in them."[197] In subsequent decades, both James and Guido punished misconduct by Polish laity through interdicts on local churches. In the first chapter of his canons of 1248, James provided that after several other steps to control a wide range of secular misbehavior, "their lands shall at once (*ex tunc*) be subject to ecclesiastical interdict, so that no ecclesiastical sacraments can be administered there beside baptism for infants and penance for the dying."[198] Nineteen years later, Guido provided for an analogous response to theft of ecclesiastical goods. "Divine services," he decreed, "shall cease in the parish in which clerical objects that have been violently removed happen to be seized or detained until restitution and worthy satisfaction."[199]

The impact of these provisions cannot be assessed; however, Pełka, James, and Guido considered them to be at least plausible deterrents. In order for suspension of sacraments to have been a plausible deterrent against the offending laymen, this social group must have routinely possessed and controlled churches, and had a vested interest, whether spiritual or financial, in their continued operation. This reading is clearly consistent with Gallus's image of the role of the "nobles" in establishing local churches in the early twelfth century, and with Pope Innocent III's brief description of the dependence of the Polish clergy on the laity in 1207. That dependence was, paradoxically, a source of control for the Polish clergy, a window for the "fear of God" that Archbishop Pełka thought the Polish military élite lacked.

By 1233, possession of churches by secular lords was routine, and so was their role in providing support to parish clergy. At the conclusion of his plan to control the proliferation of vicars in the Polish parishes, Pełka noted that "we have directed that the vicars be furnished with adequate sustenance by the lords of the churches, so that they are able to exercise hospitality and sustain themselves adequately. And we entrust the enforcement of this statute to our archdeacons."[200] Pełka recognized and accommodated the role of secular possessors of churches in their

---

[197]Ibid., no. 34 (1233), 22, lines 5–7.
[198]Ibid., no. 346 (1248), 206, lines 7–9.
[199]Ibid., 4: no. 5 (1267), 6, lines 13–14.
[200]Ibid., 2: no. 34 (1233), 23, lines 4–6.

staffing.[201] The role was limited; the lords did not, strictly speaking, select or appoint the vicars, but furnished them with suitable revenue, specifically in order for them to be able to offer one of the standard services of parish clerics, hospitality. The role was traditional, and Pełka in no sense sought to end it. It suggests that parish churches were routinely under control of secular lords, and so confirms the impressions of the earlier evidence. Pełka's answer was again to entrust the delicate task of mediating these traditional relationships to his archdeacons. Thus, ecclesiastical legislation formally devoted at least in part to control of customary secular practices relied on these practices for that very purpose.

Proliferation of clerics and competition for parishioners

Whatever the provision may or may not tell us about the effectiveness of episcopal authority over parish priests, it surely confirms the existence of parish priests, a widespread network of parishes, and recurrent experiments in bringing it under authoritative control. "Nobles," dukes, and bishops remained the essential actors in the foundation and control of parish churches from the early twelfth century well into the 1260s. After they appropriated a proportion of the existing parish churches in the twelfth and early thirteenth centuries, regular clerics became major participants in the foundation and control of parish churches. In conjunction with other evidence, the results of monastic appropriation constitute a useful additional record of the categories of clergy that supplied spiritual care, of the dynamics of demand for spiritual care, and of the implications of these issued for relationships between various categories of ecclesiastics within the archdiocese of Gniezno.

As Bishop Lawrence feared in 1217, the monastic communities in Silesia and the parish churches they appropriated faced vigorous competition for parishioners during the subsequent decades. Despite the papal prohibitions against unauthorized construction of "chapels and oratories" in the *parochiae* of the canons regular of St. Mary's and St. Vincent's in Wrocław,[202] these two houses gradually lost control over the supply of spiritual care

---

[201]Revising earlier scholarship, Wiśniowski, "Rozwój," 307, n. 41, asserts that in this clause 'domini ecclesiarum' refers to bishops, not the secular lords who possess local churches. He does not explain this revision, and in view of the otherwise clear concerns of this document and other legislation I do not accept it.

[202]Ibid., no. 60–61 (1193), 37, 40; 2: no. 397 (1250), 252, lines 26–28; 3: no. 89 (1253), 67, lines 42–44.

in the parishes they appropriated. Clerics outside the control of the canons regular acquired at least a part of the range of ritual, pastoral, and sacramental functions towards the inhabitants of the localities over which the canons regular had earlier received parochial authority; and the rights to collect a corresponding range of payments and offerings by the faithful to the clerics who performed them.[203] The canons regular vigorously contested the activities of the clerics who impinged on the areas of activity they had appropriated. The resulting conflicts spanned the several decades since the endowment of the houses until the mid-century, and were formally resolved by Pope Innocent IV in 1254 and by the papal Legate Guido in 1267.

One such conflict involved the parochial activities of the church of St. Adalbert in Wrocław, appropriated by the canons regular of St. Mary's sometime before 1148.[204] The church had acquired full parochial status some time between its appropriation and 1226, when Abbot Witosław formally renounced most of these functions, and gave them along with the church itself back to the diocese of Wrocław. That year, Bishop Lawrence noted that Witosław "gave this church into our hands with the full right of spiritual care that pertained to that church until now,"[205] and defined that "full right of spiritual care" as "baptism, visitation of the sick, burial, mortuary payment, sacrifice of the mass, and other revenues that may arise" in the settlement of Wrocław in the future.[206] However, the abbot retained some of the rights of the old parish church, including "free burial and visitation of the sick, if they are requested," and "tithes which the said church has long possessed."[207] In turn, he qualified these reservations to accommodate "the rights of those who may possess the parish up to the river" in the future.[208]

Among other things, Lawrence here provided a crisp definition of the meaning of full spiritual care and parish status in the diocese of Wrocław as of 1226. The roster of sacraments he included is commonplace, indicating that in 1226 parish status meant the

---

[203]For these payments, see Jean Coste, "L'institution paroissiale à la fin du moyen âge: approche bibliographique en vue d'enquêtes possibles," *Mélanges de l'école française de Rome*, 96 (1984): 295–326, at 318–19, 324–25. For the context of this problem, especially the existence of unattached and migratory clergy in Poland throughout the Middle Ages, see Wiśniowski, "Rozwój," 293, 305–06, and Kazimierz Nasiłowski, "Samowolne migracje kleru w świetle polskiego prawa kościelnego przed soborem trydenckim" [Voluntary migrations of the clergy in light of the Polish ecclesiastical law before the Council of Trent], *Czasopismo Prawno-Historyczne*, 11 (1959): 9–38. See also Aubrun, *La Paroisse*, 118–19.

[204]*S.U.*, 1: no. 16 (1148), 12.

[205]Ibid., no. 263 (1226), 192–93.

[206]Ibid., 193.

[207]Ibid.

[208]Ibid.

same range of spiritual functions attached to a church as it did anywhere else in Latin Europe. This is hardly surprising in view of his repeated, close involvement in establishing parishes in Silesia. However, one detail of his description seems curious. Perhaps casually, he referred to sacraments as "revenues," and thus implicitly combined their spiritual dimension with their function as sources of income. Furthermore, in the same phrase he suggested that revenues from administration of sacraments were essentially similar to revenues from tithes. This reading may be too subtle; but it does suggest that Lawrence saw definition of parish status essentially in terms of a particular set of revenues, and thought of a parish church as a bundle of rights to income no less than a source of salvation for the faithful.

Lawrence and Witosław anticipated the formation of new parishes and tithe revenues in Wrocław. Lawrence implied that had the canons not given up the church of St. Adalbert and the functions it had performed as of 1226, that church would have served as a parish center for that expanding population. The abbot was reluctant to take on that role. Perhaps, like Archpriest Siebracht of Krosno in the same year, he found the prospect too burdensome. However, in contrast to Siebracht, he did not take on other priests to staff the church, but renounced it and its spiritual functions altogether, retaining solely its oldest and most traditional spiritual functions and obligations. These included the earliest tithe revenues—expressly not tithe revenues from recent and anticipated settlement—and care of the sick and dying and of the dead, next to baptism the core area of sacramental care.[209] Lawrence and Witosław turned the old parish church into a position of formal, residual seniority among the anticipated parish churches of Wrocław. The status they envisioned for it in 1226 was comparable to the minster or baptismal churches elsewhere in Europe which formally retained their most ancient and fundamental spiritual rights while in effect ceasing to perform any spiritual functions in practice.

A few days later, Bishop Lawrence in turn transferred the church of St. Adalbert "in the city" to the newly arrived community of Preachers, the first established in Silesia.[210] At the trans-

---

[209]The other such area was baptism; see Aubrun, La Paroisse, 96: "C'est la concession d'un cimetière à une chapelle qui la promeut au rang d'église paroissiale, tout autant que l'attribution des fonts baptismaux."

[210]S.U., 1: no. 266 (1226), 195; on the background, see Jerzy Kłoczowski, Dominikanie polscy na Śląsku w XIII–XIV wieku [Polish Dominicans in Silesia in the thirteenth-fourteenth centuries] (Lublin, 1956); idem, "Dominicans of the Polish Province in the Middle Ages," in Kłoczowski, Christian Community, 73–118; Silnicki, Dzieje, 388–89.

fer, he emphatically disclaimed any intention to subject the friars to any obligations of spiritual care. "Born from our loins and suckled at our breasts with the milk of liberty," the friars were "to be immune from every concern of cure of souls," and were merely to "lead our people to salvation by word and example," that is, to preach.[211] Lawrence's disclaimer seems an extraordinary lapse into ambivalence about the whole project of providing and expanding spiritual care by a bishop as thoroughly engaged in it as Lawrence was. He did not merely describe spiritual care as alien to the mendicants' function—this would have been a familiar formulation of functions appropriate for different orders of clergy—but described administration of spiritual care as a positive burden, and exemption from it as an immunity, a form of freedom, and a display of maternal love for a child. His words anticipate the slightly colder concerns of Polish and Italian prelates about clerical avoidance of pastoral responsibilities through uncontrolled proliferation of vicars and vicars' vicars.

Lawrence carved out some exceptions to that favor, and in turn described them as favors. The friars did not have to perform any spiritual functions at all "unless it pleases the brothers at some time to visit the sick as a work of mercy."[212] He also "crowned with a privilege of security" the burial rights (sepulturam) "which have until now pertained to it [i.e., the church of St. Adalbert's for the faithful] from everywhere."[213] These two exceptions—visitations of the sick and burial rights—were the areas of spiritual authority Abbot Witosław had reserved for the church of St. Adalbert a few days earlier. Of these two functions, the friars clearly acquired the right to visit the sick and dying. The old parish church was presumably to serve as the base from which they would venture on their visits. Lawrence did not expressly grant the friars the burial rights of the church of St. Adalbert's; perhaps Abbot Witosław and his canons regular retained them. However, in view of the overall thrust of transferring the reserved core of spiritual functions to the friars, I would guess that they acquired that function as well. If so, then over the few days in 1226 the friars acquired an option to visit the sick and dying, administer the last rites, bury the dead in their cemetery, and collect the corresponding range of fees. All these functions were, however,

---

[211]S.U., 1: no. 266 (1226), 195. For the broad definition of that expression, including preaching but not limited to it, see Caroline Walker Bynum, *Docere Verbo et Exemplo: An Aspect of Twelfth-Century Spirituality* (Harvard Theological Studies, No. 31. Missoula, Mont., 1979).

[212]S.U., 1: no. 266 (1226), 195.

[213]Ibid.

voluntary on both sides; the friars were to perform them if they were solicited, and if they wished to respond.

The events of 1226 involved several categories of clergy: the chapter of Wrocław; the monastic community of St. Mary's; and the friars. The bishop and chapter appropriated the old parish church of St. Adalbert, and transferred it to the friars, minus most of its parish functions. What happened to these functions? Were the parish functions of St. Adalbert's eliminated altogether? If not, who performed them? During the subsequent decades, succession to the parochial rights of St. Adalbert's led to conflict between the canons regular of St. Mary's and priests of the new parish churches established in Wrocław after 1226, as was expected.

Despite Abbot Witosław's resignation from most parochial functions and rights in 1226, the canons regular of St. Mary's continued to perform a wide range of spiritual and pastoral activities within the expanding urban region. Their activities collided with the interests of the parish churches of St. Mary Magdalen's and St. Elisabeth's that had been established in Wrocław after 1226.[214] The ensuing conflict between canons regular and the parish clergy lasted until Legate Guido resolved the claims in 1267. During his visit, Guido was approached by "Hartwig, canon and rector of the church of St. Mary Magdalen's of Wrocław," who asserted that the canons regular of St. Mary's "were visiting the sick, hearing confessions, giving Eucharist, removing the bodies of the dead and burying them at their monastery, and that they administered other ecclesiastical sacraments within his parish against his will and to the prejudice of the parish church."[215] Hartwig based his claims on Abbot Witosław's abdication of parochial functions and rights over the church of St. Adalbert in 1226. As far as he was concerned, the parish of St. Mary Magdalen's was the formal successor to the functions and rights of St. Adalbert's. The canons regular disagreed, and evidently considered themselves successors to the rights of the old church they had once possessed.

Hartwig demanded that the canons regular cease performing the controverted spiritual functions, and that they pay his parish substantial damages. He "requested to be compensated . . . from the proceeds at [a level of] up to 20 silver marks, and that the said

---

[214]For the distribution of the parish churches of St. Mary Magdalen's, St. Elisabeth's, and several other parish churches in the expanding suburb of Wrocław, see the maps in Wędzki, "Wrocław," 605–07, and Młynarska-Kaletynowa, Wrocław, 45, 122, 139.

[215]S.U., 4: no. 12 (1267), 13, lines 43–44, and 14, lines 1–4.

abbot and brothers desist from the said [activities]."[216] Ironically, it was the canons regular who used Abbot Witosław's 1226 alienation of parochial rights of St. Adalbert's as a defense against Hartwig's claim. Guido's compromise closely followed the terms of the documents of 1226. "Since we note," he wrote,[217]

two exceptions in the exchange [made by] the said bishop, abbot, and brothers, free burial and visitation of the sick, if they are requested [to perform it] we pronounce, by the will of the parties who have submitted themselves to our decree, that the said abbot and brothers of St. Mary are permitted to visit the sick and may acquire the bodies of the dead from the parish of St. Mary Magdalen, save for the parochial right and the canonical portion due to the said parish priest, if they are requested [to pay it]. [As compensation] for the gains received, the said abbot and brothers shall pay the said Hartwig 4 silver marks of common weight.

Guido sought to ensure that the canons regular would read this exception strictly; he "prohibit[ed] the said canons from presuming to administer sacraments other than the said [two] in this parish in the future."[218] In this sense, the new town parish achieved a favorable reading of the grant of 1226, though not the blanket prohibition of spiritual competence Hartwig seemed to ask for. In addition, the fine imposed on the canons was substantial. Though it was far from the level Hartwig had sought from the canons regular in damages, the fine did place the house in a state of debt. Guido provided that the four marks were to be paid "before Easter," and noted that the "said abbot had placed himself under obligation to pay them, and promised again before us to pay them prior to the said term."[219] Thus, while the resolution was a compromise between claims of the two sides, the canons regular suffered the clearer loss. It appears that in competition between the relatively old, monastic possessors of parochial functions and new parishes the legate was quite responsive to the claims of the latter.

The other conflict concerned a relatively narrow, non-sacramental issue. In 1267, Legate Guido noted that there had been a conflict between "the religious [men], abbot and convent of St. Mary . . . in Wrocław . . . and the . . . parish priests of the churches of St. Mary Magdalen and St. Elisabeth of this city" concerning benediction of candles and palm branches for the faithful

---

[216]Ibid, no. 12 (1267), 14, lines 4–5.
[217]Ibid, lines 9–16.
[218]Ibid, lines 17–18.
[219]Ibid, lines 15–17.

during Easter.[220] Guido accommodated the roles of both the house and the two parishes involved, and the parishioners' choice of the place where the blessings took place. He implied that on this occasion the parties were relatively easy to reconcile. He noted that[221]

the case between [the parishes and the canons regular] was peaceably closed in this way. The said parish priests of St. Mary Magdalen and St. Elisabeth shall from now on bless candles on [the day of] the Purification of the Holy Virgin and [palm] branches on Palm Sunday, without contradiction by the said abbot and convent, while the said parish priests shall henceforth not impede . . . any of their parishioners so [that each of them] can . . . freely and fully go to the said church of St. Mary the Virgin for candles and [palm] branches to be blessed.

Guido fairly carefully allowed all the concerned religious institutions this particular function; he also explicitly allowed parishioners a choice of place where the function took place. This compromise was not contingent on consent by either party to the performance of the cult by the other, nor did it involve any compensation to either side. It seems that in this case, where the subject of the conflict was much narrower than sacramental functions, the parties were relatively amenable to compromise, and an element of cult was expressly allowed in more than one place.

The canons regular of St. Vincent's also faced competition for parishioners within the region in which they had appropriated local churches before 1201. The number of the local churches under their spiritual supervision did not change between 1201 and the mid-century.[222] However, the canons lost effective control over the clergy who performed spiritual care in their *parochia*, and, evidently, over construction of the local churches staffed by that clergy. In 1254, Pope Innocent IV explained the details of the competition for parishioners within the *parochia* of St. Vincent's in considerable detail. He described the control the canons had enjoyed over the churches since 1201, the interference with that control, and the impact of that interference on the material revenues of the appropriated churches and of the canons' community. Between 1201 and the middle of the century the canons had routinely selected the parish priests of the appropriated

---

[220]Ibid, no. 9 (1267), 12, lines 1–4.
[221]Ibid, no. 9 (1267), 12, lines 4–10.
[222]Ibid., 3: no. 89 (1253), 67, lines 9–11.

churches. The canons informed the pope that "they had assigned priests to hear confessions of their parishioners in the churches that belong . . . to them."[223] In 1254, Innocent noted that the canons were especially skilled in selecting priests "who know how to lead the sick minds of the mortals to salvation through divine care and by pious moderation, according to age, sex, and strength."[224] He did not explain whether this comment was his own gloss or whether it was part of the canons' assertion. In any event, it is clear that the pope fully subscribed to the canons' claim of unique qualification to select the personnel that administered spiritual care.

Control over spiritual care by the canons regular had suffered because of interference of "certain religious men" (*quidam religiosi*) with the inhabitants formally served by the appropriated local churches. Pope Innocent did not expressly identify who these "religious men" were. The term suggests that he was referring to regular clerics, that is, monks, canons regular, or friars.[225] In two clauses of the letter, he clearly referred to the offenders as regular clerics. He directed the whole complaint against "religious men of whatever order"; and expressed a wish "that all the faithful in Christ especially the adherents to the regular order be so governed by the exertion of wisdom that no curious observer may find anything [suspiciously] noteworthy among them."[226] The pope did not state which order, or orders, supplied the clerics who competed with the parish priests licitly selected by the canons. The contemporary context offers several possibilities but no way to choose between them. The competing clerics may have been selected by the monks and nuns of the Cistercian houses in Lubiąż, Trzebnica, and Henryków. In particular, the network of parishes recorded in the estate of the monks of Lubiąż in 1202 and 1217 was situated in the same region of settlement as was the *parochia* of the canons regular of St. Vincent's. Thus, the source of competition might have been the priests appointed by the monks of Lubiąż for their appropriated churches or by the other monastic and canonical communities that had been established in Silesia during the preceding half-century. Or the monks themselves could have ministered to the population settled in the region.

---

[223]Ibid., no. 121 (1254), 87, lines 9–10.

[224]Ibid., lines 10–11.

[225]For the standard meaning of *religiosi*, see Richard Southern, *Western Society and Church in the Middle Ages* (Harmondsworth, 1970), 214. For the possibilities of what he may have meant, see Nasiłowski, "Samowolne migracje," 9–16, 23, 37–38. Aubrun, *La Paroisse*, 119, 122–26.

[226]*S.U.*, 3: no. 121 (1254), 87, lines 44–45.

Finally, the newly established mendicants could have competed with the older parishes, despite Bishop Lawrence's earlier portrayals of this function as a burden for them.[227]

It seems in any case that the grievance dealt with categories of offending clerics other than parish priests who had been appointed by monastic communities situated near one another, and who impinged on each other's spiritual and pastoral activities. Pope Innocent pointedly noted that the offending clerics had neither authority nor competence to administer sacraments. He remarked that "these religious men are unable to loose or bind because they are not the judges" of the parishioners, that as a result the absolution they purport to offer the parishioners is "pretended," and that they consign the souls of the parishioners and their own souls to "a quick damnation."[228] Innocent thus implied that they lacked orders of priesthood altogether.

In addition to their formal invalidity, the sacraments fraudulently administered by these clerics represented an inadequate level of pastoral care. At least as the abbot had alleged it, the competing clerics performed their spiritual functions badly because of their unfamiliarity with the parishioners. They claimed that the clerics whom they had not appointed did not "know how to lead the sick minds of the mortals to salvation by divine care [and] in pious moderation, according to age, sex, and strength," and, "out of ignorance of [the parishioners'] spiritual features, could not give a worthy reason for this [pretended absolution] or furnish salutary remedies for those entrusted to [their] care," because they were "unaware of [their] sickness and circumstances."[229] The spiritual care administered by the usurping clerics was therefore invalidated by formal as well as practical inadequacy. Finally, the illicit activities of the "religious men" resulted in financial loss to the parish priests who had been licitly appointed by the abbot and canons regular of St. Vincent's. "These religious men," the pope continued, "entice parishioners with great damage to the others, and . . . as a result the said

---

[227] On the role of mendicants, particularly Dominicans, in the administration of sacraments in Silesia during the thirteenth century, see Kłoczowski, Dominikanie polscy, 252–71, and idem, "Dominicans," 84–85; see also Aubrun, La Paroisse, 123–25. Kłoczowski notes the earliest papal resolutions of conflicts among parish clergy and the mendicants between the 1280s and the Council of Vienne, and thus quite late; Dominikanie polscy, 256–61. Nevertheless, the detail and complexity of the resolutions he cites suggest that such conflicts were not new.

[228] S.U., 3: no. 121 (1254), 87, lines 14–15, 18.

[229] Ibid., lines 10–11, 20–22.

abbot and convent, and the rectors of the said churches [appointed by the canons] are defrauded by diverse ways of the usual offerings and incidents of their parishioners."[230]

These complaints imply that the pool of clerics from which the usurpers were selected was broad, and that the categories included clerics with and without priestly orders. Perhaps the diversity of sources of spiritual care, licit or illicit, is more important than the precise identification of the source of spiritual competition that triggered the abbot's complaint. A story recorded in the Life of St. Hedwig of Silesia later seems to confirm the proliferation of clerics who could potentially have exercised priestly functions illicitly or licitly in central Silesia during her lifetime. The story is apocryphal and didactic; whether or not the narrated events took place, the narrative at least reflects a concern with accurate identification of those clerics who were specifically authorized to perform priestly functions, among other categories of clergy.

One of the distinctive features of Duchess Hedwig's piety was her insistence on large numbers of priests to celebrate mass for her.[231] Her hagiographer noted that "when any priests came to her court, whether they were secular [clerics] or religious [men], they were hardly allowed to leave until they read mass before her."[232] At its most conservative reading the passage presumes that there were at least two categories of clerics with priestly orders in central Silesia around the mid-thirteenth century. They included both secular clerics and the "religious men." The latter category corresponds to the clerics against whom Innocent IV expressly directed his letter. Both types of clerics were evidently quite mobile; they visited the duchess's court in substantial numbers. The hagiographer does not relate their periodic appearances at her court to any spiritual functions they may also have performed in local churches. At the least, however, their periodic travel to her court suggests that they rather actively sought places or contexts within which to exercise spiritual care, in addition to or perhaps instead of staffing parish churches. These routine appearances of priests at her court caused considerable irritation among Hedwig's court chaplains and officials. This group was disturbed with the frequency of the masses, and with the

---

[230]Ibid., lines 27–31.

[231]Vauchez, La saintété, 432–33.

[232]M.P.H., 4: 539: "Quicumque ad eius curiam presbiteri venebant, sive seculares essent sive religiosi, vix umquam evadere poterant quin eos coram ea missam legere oporteret."

recruitment of large numbers of priests to celebrate them.[233] The resentment at court may have been another area of competition among various categories of clerics over the performance of priestly functions.

Despite her court clergy, Duchess Hedwig actively sought to attract and keep substantial groups of these itinerant priests at court at any one time. "If," the hagiographer narrates, "at some time the large supply of priests diminished, she summoned [a priest] from wherever one could be procured in order to make up for the scarcity of masses, which she was unable to sustain without displeasure."[234] On one occasion, her attempt at procuring a priest led to serious confusion. The reasons for, and results of, that confusion illustrate the diversity of clerics in central Silesia around the mid-thirteenth century, and the resulting potential for the blurring of distinctions between their categories and areas of competence. Hedwig sent out her chaplain, Martin, "to fetch some priest who would read mass to her."[235] A bit sheepishly, Martin proceeded to carry out her order. "Compelled by the command—which it did not behoove him to contradict—he went off, albeit reluctantly,"[236] but he carried out his mission carelessly. Whether out of spite or negligence, he solicited the clearly wrong category of cleric for the services demanded by the duchess. "By accident, he met a certain bald lay brother (*conversus*) on his way to the duke's court on some business, took him with himself, and presented him to the duchess."[237]

What ensued illustrates the confusion between different categories of clerics and clerical roles, and for deliberate misrepresentation of these roles to persons who sought spiritual services from priests. Hedwig failed to distinguish the lay brother from a priest. "Since she was [a person] of admirable simplicity, she thought that he was not a lay brother by vocation, but merely bald. Thinking that he was a priest, she . . . requested him to read the mass out to her."[238] Though the hagiographer clearly considered Hedwig's inability to differentiate between a lay brother and an ordained priest as a stereotyped model of her saintly innocence, in order for that particular event to be a cred-

---

[233]The hagiographer notes that "the chaplains and [court] servitors were bothered by the frequency of the masses," and reports that "a certain cleric" composed an ironic poem about this unusual manifestation of religiosity. Ibid.

[234]Ibid.

[235]Ibid.

[236]Ibid.

[237]Ibid.

[238]Ibid.

ible illustration of the model, these two very different categories of cleric must in fact have been quite similar. In the ordinary circumstances, tonsure must have been the clearest visual distinction between a priest and a lay brother. The passage implies that the lay brother was ordinarily tonsured, but that, for obvious reasons, that distinguishing feature was unavailable when either category of cleric—ordained priest or lay brother—was bald.

When he realized why Chaplain Martin had brought him before Duchess Hedwig, the bald lay brother vigorously declined to say mass for her, declaring himself incompetent. "Astonished, he announced that he was neither a priest nor instructed in letters. The lady noticed the deception, [but] recognized that he had not done this by [intent of] a ridiculing soul but out of ignorance, and humbly begged the man's pardon."[239] Hedwig realized that her mistake had been Martin's fault, either by carelessness or by design. Nevertheless, she chastised Martin gently, affording for the hagiographer a stereotypical model of gentleness and forgiveness. "With a sweet leniency, she said to the chaplain, 'May God spare you for deceiving me like that.' "[240] The effect for the hagiographer is a literary story of a cycle of noble innocence, deception, and forgiveness. However, the events and processes with reference to which this cycle was expressed shed some light on the institutional context within which the conventional traits were imagined as operating.

The story clearly assumes that around the middle of the thirteenth century there was a fairly wide array of clerics who either did or plausibly could perform priestly services in Silesia, that these clerics impinged on each other's activities, and that the results caused some resentment among several categories of clerics. At least three categories of clerics were ordained to perform priestly functions: the secular clergy, "religious men," and chaplains who performed services for the rulers at their courts. In addition, it was potentially plausible for other, non-ordained clerics to exercise priestly functions. These categories of clerics seem to have played rather complicated roles. The priests spent at least some of their time traveling to the ducal court to perform masses, in addition to, or instead of, whatever activity they carried out in local churches. Overall, this clergy was mobile, busy, and sharply competitive. Performance of priestly activities was one focus of their diverse activity and competition.

---

[239]Ibid.
[240]Ibid.

The abbot alleged that the offending clerics officiated in their own churches, which had been "established against the decrees of the holy canons."[241] The number of these churches is entirely undocumented, but the allegation may explain Pope Innocent's reminder against construction of unauthorized "chapels and oratories" a year earlier. "The parishioners," added the pontiff, "hear the voice of the priests in the said churches, at divine offices as well as in utterance of holy preaching."[242] In addition, the clerics heard confession and administered Eucharist.[243] The pope was especially disturbed by the fact that the parishioners were exercising choice of place where they heard mass and sermons. Specifically in this context, he asserted that the parishioners were going to the churches where the unauthorized priests officiated in order to "hear the offices according to their own free will."[244] The availability of choice of spiritual care to parishioners was wholly undesirable. In this sense, Pope Innocent's document reflects an underlying competition for parishioners among different potential providers of spiritual care.

Competition for parishioners between the licit and illicit clerics was especially acute with respect to spiritual care for the sick and dying. The prospect of a parishioner's death raised a flurry of activity concerning the disposal of his or her material possessions, body, and soul. According to the pope,[245]

this abbot and convent also added that when [one of] the parishioners of the churches [appropriated by the canons] falls into bed with an illness, the said religious men immediately assemble, visit the ill parishioner uninvited, under guise of piety, [and try] to compose and arrange his will, and to assume the . . . honor of becoming executors of his will. What else? Lured by their flattering sermons, the ill [parishioners] disregard [their] ancestral and paternal graves, and their ample bequests [to the deceiving churches] grow, while [their bequests] to the said churches [appropriated by the canons] are nonexistent or small.

The impending death of a parishioner gave rise to a curious spectacle involving the bedridden ill and groups of "religious men." These clerics were uninvited; thus, they did not wait to be summoned to the bedside of the ill person, but instead relied on some other source of information that a death was impending. Their

---

[241]Ibid., line 26.
[242]S.U., 3: no. 121 (1254), 87, lines 23–26.
[243]Ibid.
[244]Ibid., line 27.
[245]Ibid., lines 31–37.

unsolicited convergence in groups suggests that they kept each other closely informed about the state of health of the population in each appropriated parish. Once in the presence of the sick or dying parishioner, they sought to affect the most thorough possible disposal of his or her inheritance in the broadest sense. Competition for parishioners became competition for physical control over the parishioners' bodies and estates.

As the abbot saw it, the resulting pressure by "religious men" was sufficiently effective to snatch a substantial proportion of dead bodies away from the cemeteries in which the inhabitants of each locality were traditionally buried (and which had been licitly appropriated by the canons), and to remove a substantial proportion of the material part of the decedents' estates. The loss of revenues from burials and from payments that had been levied for the execution of wills was sufficiently high to finance construction of the illicit churches from which the "religious men" operated. "Since," the complaint continued, "the said abbot, convent, and [their licitly appointed] rectors are unable to exact a canonical portion out of these bequests, . . . these [illicit] clerics procure these [revenues] through theft, [and use them] for the construction of their [own] churches and for [support of] . . . divine veneration [there]."[246]

If the abbot's complaint was at least largely accurate, then the activities of the usurping "religious men" in defiance of the canons regular were sufficiently entrenched to be financially self-sustaining. The "religious men" served as parish clergy through the full cycle of pastoral, sacramental, financial, and church-building activity. Although from the canons' perspective they were clearly usurpers, their presence between 1201 and 1254 clearly thickens the network of local churches and the availability of spiritual care in central Silesia considerably beyond that appropriated by the major monastic communities in the early thirteenth century.

The remedies the pope outlined in response to the illicit activities of the "religious men" were broadly prohibitory and severe in tone, but moderate in substance. Innocent accommodated part of the controverted practices, and further implied that these practices had at least arguably been permissible local arrangements rather than usurpations. In addition, he relied on Polish bishops to carry out the sanctions. He mandated the archbishop of Gniezno and his suffragans to prohibit the parishioners from

---

[246]Ibid., lines 37–40.

soliciting pastoral and spiritual care from the illicit "religious men," and to prohibit these "religious men" from offering pastoral and spiritual care to the parishioners. The parishioners were to be compelled to "spurn the said churches," and "not to approach churches other [than the parish churches appropriated by the canons] in order to hear divine office and receive ecclesiastical sacraments."[247] Likewise, the "religious men" were to be compelled "not to receive the said parishioners to these sorts of offices or sacraments, with prejudice to others, or to hear confessions."[248] Both sides were to be deterred by the threat of ecclesiastical censure. The pope's mandate was intended to override any arrangements to the contrary that may have been worked out to accommodate the controverted activities of the "religious men" over the preceding half century. "You shall compel," he wrote to the bishops,[249]

[the parishioners and clerics] by ecclesiastical censure, without [exception on account of any] previous reason or regard for any indulgence for these or other religious men, expressed in form of words [and] granted by the apostolic see, because of which . . . they might cause the present writing, set out explicitly word for word, to be obscured or disturbed.

This complicated conclusion of the letter suggests that although in the course of the conflict which culminated in 1254 the activities of the "religious men" were explicitly declared illicit, during the preceding half-century these activities had in fact enjoyed some kind of formal sanction that could at least have been argued in response to the canons' claim to exclusive control over parish clergy within their *parochia*. The pope obliquely referred to that sanction as "previous reason" and an "indulgence," by which he presumably meant special permission to carry out otherwise illicit or sinful activity.[250] It had been approved by previous popes, and presumably the Polish episcopate. These sources of plausible authorization for activities of the "religious men" suggest that they were not usurpers at all, but rather that between 1201 and 1254 there had been a proliferation of licit but competing pastoral and sacramental care in central Silesia, and that the ecclesiastical

---

[247]Ibid., lines 48–49.

[248]Ibid., 87, line 4988, line 1.

[249]Ibid., 88, lines 6–9: "per censuram ecclesiasticam appellatione remota previa ratione compellens, non obstante aliqua indulgentia religiosis ipsis vel aliis sub quacumque forma verborum ab apostolica sede concessa per quam non expressam presentibus de verbo ad verbum premissa impediri valeant vel differi."

[250]For the meaning of the term as a special grant or concession, see Niermeyer, p. 528, s.v. *indulgentia*, variant 6.

institutions that had suffered a net loss of control over that care as a result, that is, the major monastic communities claimed usurpation in order to regain their previously exclusive rights.

Notably, they failed to recover these rights. Although Pope Innocent invalidated any past authorization to the "religious men" for engaging in pastoral and sacramental activities, his actual remedies did not prohibit these activities, but on the contrary accommodated their continued performance. He qualified the invalidation with a yawning exception; he provided that[251]

these religious men . . . shall not receive the . . . parishioners to . . . offices and sacraments . . . or hear confessions, unless permission is sought and received beforehand from [their] own priests, according to the statutes of the general council. And they [the religious men] shall accept them [the parishioners] for burial at their [cemetery] only if they [the parishioners] choose to be buried there by devotion of their soul, provided however that . . . that church [which loses burial rights] shall not be defrauded of [its] canonical portion.

These exceptions clearly assume that the "religious men" would remain active within the old *parochia* of St. Vincent's, and expressly permitted the parishioners to solicit their pastoral and sacramental services—subject, however, to consent from the parish clergy appointed by the canons, and to remuneration of that clergy for loss of revenue. Thus, far from abolishing the diversity of spiritual services and activities within the parishes appropriated by the canons between 1201 and 1254, Innocent recognized and assumed future coexistence and ongoing competition within the complex network of clerics, and limited the remedies specifically to accommodate the financial interests threatened by the competition. What formally began as a sharp condemnation of the proliferating activity of clerics within the local society encompassed by the *parochia* of St. Vincent's after the turn of the thirteenth century, by the 1250s became a formula for ordered institutional coexistence within that society, a multiplicity of sources of spiritual care, and piecemeal adjustments of the resulting flow of revenues.

---

[251]*S.U.*, 3: no. 121 (1254), 87, line 4988, line 4: "necnon et ipsos religiosos cuiuscumque sint ordinis ne in aliorum preiudicium parrochianos prefatos ad huiusmodi officia seu sacramenta recipiant nec confessiones audiant eorundem nisi petita prius et obtenta licentia a sacerdote proprio iuxta statuta concilii generalis nec etiam nisi apud eos ex devotione animi elegerint tumulari ipsos ad sepulturant admittant, ita tamen quod tunc eedem ecclesie portione canonica non fraudentur."

3. CLERGY AND TRANSFER OF TITHE REVENUES

Transfer of tithe revenues: the roles of bishop and chapter

Next to the "noble" and the ruler, the anonymous twelfth-century chronicler rather obliquely referred to a cleric as an actor in the creation of the local church built by the "noble." He noted that the church was consecrated, and then moved on to another subject.[252] His is the earliest hint of the central role of bishops in the foundation and endowment of local churches. Later documents show that the bishops and cathedral canons were crucial actors in this process throughout the period under study. Bishops consecrated churches. The vast majority of the documents recording transfer of tithe revenue to new possessors were written by bishops, witnessed by their chapter, and validated by the seals of the bishop and of the chapter.[253] Bishops were also authors of all documents that granted or confirmed parochial status of local churches.[254] Although dukes and other laymen were among tithe possessors, documents recording the transfers of tithes were either issued by bishops and chapter, or acknowledged a role of bishops and chapter in their alienation.[255]

In addition, bishops and cathedral canons remained the single most important category of possessors of tithes well into the thirteenth century, ever since Pope Innocent II vested the Polish

---

[252]*M.P.H.*, 1: 449, lines 10–14.

[253]The frequency of the formal traces of ecclesiastical involvement varied over time and between different episcopates on which see below, but the documents clearly show that the essential donor of tithe revenues was the bishop and chapter. See *S.U.*,1: no. 56 (1170–89), 32–33; no. 57 (1189), 33–34; no. 82 (1202), 54; no. 88 (1203), 61; no. 89 (1203), 61–62; no. 122 (1210), 88–89; no. 129 (1212), 94; no. 143 (1214), 101–02; no. 171 (1218), 123–26; no. 182 (1218), 135–36; no. 186 (1219), 138; no. 195 (1220), 144; no. 198 (1220), 146–47; no. 209 (1221), 152–53; no. 226 (1223), 164–66; no. 237 (1223), 172–73; no. 240 (1223), 175; no. 270 (1226), 198–99; no. 282 (1227), 208; no. 283 (1227), 208–09; no. 285 (1228), 210; no. 306 (1229), 226; 2: no. 2 (1231), 1–2; no. 21 (1232), 11–12; no. 60 (1234), 38; no. 125 (1236), 82; no. 138 (1237), 90; no. 176 (1240), 113; no. 183 (1240), 116–17; no. 195 (1240), 123; no. 279 (1244), 167–68; 3: no. 2 (1251–62), 15–16; no. 5 (1251), 17; no. 6 (1251), 17–18; no. 136 (1254), 90; no. 144 (1255), 101–02; no. 181 (1257), 124–25; no. 358 (1261), 233–34; no. 361 (1261), 235; no. 387 (1262), 259–60.

[254]Ibid., 1: no. 156–57 (1217), 113–14; no. 256 (1226), 187; no. 257 (1226), 187–88; no. 258 (1226), 188–89; no. 263 (1226), 192–93; no. 266 (1226), 194–95.

[255]Ibid., no. 77 (1202), 49–51; no. 83 (1202–03), 54–58; no. 114–15 (1226), 79–85; no. 226 (1223), 164–66.

episcopate with possession of tithe revenues in the archdiocese of Gniezno in 1136.[256] The transfers of tithe revenue from prior ecclesiastical possessors entailed rather elaborate and formal adjustments of vested rights, and preventions or resolutions of several kinds of conflict. The episcopal documents shed light on the processes within clerical groups that effected these alienations, on the relative importance of bishops and the clerics divested of tithe revenue, and on the initiatives for and consent to the transfers within ecclesiastical groups.[257]

The bishop was the most important cleric concerned with the transfer of tithe revenues throughout the period under study. Nearly all of the episcopal documents recording transfers of revenue carry the bishop's seal. In a formal sense, the chapter seems less important; the charters begin to carry the seal of the chapter between twenty and thirty years after the seal of the bishop appears, and then rather intermittently until the later part of the episcopate of Bishop Thomas after the mid-thirteenth century.[258] No document refers to a seal representing both bishop and chapter. The chapter was, however, important in several other ways. The charters record consent of the chapter to tithe transfers ever since the start; that consent is recorded as frequently as the bishop's seal, but became less frequent during Bishop Thomas's episcopate.[259]

With the same frequency, the charters in addition specify the actual canons who were present at the transfers.[260] These groups of canons varied rather widely from one occasion to another.

[256]V.-W., 3–8.

[257]On these subjects in general, see Szymański, "Biskupstwa," 178–231; Silnicki, Dzieje, 74–84, 324–55; Stanisław Zachorowski, Rozwój i ustrój kapituł polskich w wiekach średnich [Development and structure of the Polish chapters in the Middle Ages] (Kraków, 1912), especially 60–69, 80–94, 131–49, 218–28; Brian Tierney, Foundations of the Conciliar Theory: The Contribution of the Medieval Canonists from Gratian to the Great Schism (Cambridge, 1955, repr. 1968), 106–32; Lawrence G. Duggan, Bishop and Chapter: The Governance of the Bishopric of Speyer to 1552 (New Brunswick, N.J., 1978), 11–56.

[258]S.U., 1: no. 129 (1212), 94; no. 171 (1218), 123–26; no. 195 (1220), 144; no. 226 (1223), 164–66; no. 237 (1223), 172–73; no. 270 (1226), 198–99; no. 282 (1227), 208; no. 283 (1227), 208–09; no. 306 (1229), 226; no. 60 (1234), 38; no. 125 (1236), 82; no. 138 (1237), 90; no. 176 (1240), 113; 3: no. 5 (1251), 17; no. 6 (1251), 17–18; no. 144 (1255), 101–02; no. 181 (1257), 124–25; no. 358 (1261), 233–34; no. 361 (1261), 235; no. 387 (1262), 259–60.

[259]Ibid., 1: no. 56 (1170–89), 32–33; no. 57 (1189), 33–34; no. 88 (1203), 61; no. 122 (1210), 88–89; no. 129 (1212), 94; no. 171 (1218), 123–26; no. 182 (1218), 135–36; no. 209 (1221), 152–53; no. 226 (1223), 164–66; no. 237 (1223), 172–73; no. 240 (1223), 175; no. 270 (1226), 198–99; no. 283 (1227), 208–09; no. 285 (1228), 210; no. 306 (1229), 226; 2: no. 21 (1232), 11–12; no. 138 (1237), 90; no. 176 (1240), 113; 3: no. 2 (1251–62), 15–16; no. 5 (1251), 17; no. 358 (1261), 233–34; no. 361 (1261), 235; no. 387 (1262), 259–60.

[260]Ibid., 1: no. 57 (1189), 33–34; no. 82 (1202), 54; no. 122 (1210), 88–89; no. 129 (1212), 94; no. 143 (1214), 101–02; no. 171 (1218), 123–26; no. 186 (1219), 138; no. 198 (1220), 146–47; no. 226 (1223), 164–66; no. 237 (1223), 172–73; no. 240 (1223), 175; no. 270 (1226), 198–99; no.

Their core, however, always consisted of the chapter officials, most frequently the dean, archdeacon, provost, chancellor, scholar, custodian, and chanter. Quite early in the period spanned by the documentation, the bishops recognized that this group sufficed to express meaningful consent on behalf of the chapter. In 1189, Bishop Żyrosław validated transfer of a church at Bardo and its tithe revenue "by counsel and consent of the major persons of the chapter of Wrocław."[261] In 1203 Bishop Cyprian used the same words to approve of the gift of tithes of lord Emmeram's church at Strzegom, and in 1221 Pope Honorius III similarly described consent of the chapter to a gift of tithes for a community of canons regular in Naumburg.[262]

A substantial proportion of these charters also record the clergy directly affected by loss of tithe revenue. On a few occasions, the recorded clerics are parish priests. In most cases, however, they were cathedral canons. There is in fact close correspondence between the persons listed in attendance at the transfers and the persons who lost tithe revenue. On occasion, the clerics present at the transfers were witnesses to transfers that affected their own revenue. More frequently, the persons in attendance during particular transfers were themselves possessors of tithe revenues, and lost them on other occasions. Taken over time, the confrontation of canons listed as witnesses with canons deprived of tithe revenue suggests that they are the same people, and that alienation of tithe revenue to new, monastic possessors was a self-dealing affair by the canons as a group. The bishop and chapter thus did not simply consent to transfer of tithe revenues; every time they approved of a transfer, they sacrificed a part of the revenues of the canons. Upon a transfer, the clerics deprived of tithe revenue were usually offered compensation, either in the form of tithe revenue from other localities, or in the form of some other revenue.

Cathedral canons were the most conspicuous parties to the endowment of monastic communities with tithe revenue. Beneath the formally collective actions of the chapter, expressed through the seal, consent, and witness of "major persons," alienations of tithe revenues entailed initiatives of specific canons, and concerned their individual prebends. On one occasion in 1189,

---

283 (1227), 208–09; no. 285 (1228), 210; no. 306 (1229), 226; 2: no. 2 (1231), 1–2; no. 60 (1234), 38; no. 176 (1240), 113; 3: no. 2 (1251–62), 15–16; no. 5 (1251), 17; no. 358 (1261), 233–34; no. 361 (1261), 235; no. 387 (1262), 259–60.

[261]Ibid., no. 57 (1189), 33.

[262]Ibid., no. 88 (1203), 61; no. 204 (1221), 150.

Bishop Żyrosław nicely expressed the alienation of tithe revenue as both a collective activity of the chapter and a source of spiritual reward for its individual members. After prefacing his grant of tithes to the Hospitallers with acknowledgment of "counsel and consent of the major persons of the chapter of Wrocław," he noted an agreement between "us" and the monks, "that whenever one of our canons dies, they shall celebrate his obsequy— that is an obsequy for each brother—and shall send his written death notice to Jerusalem."[263] The chapter was associated with the gifts in a way that reflected both its collective institutional identity and the desire of its individual members for salvation. The ultimate beneficiaries of transfer of tithe revenue were the individual canons.

The roles of individual canons in the transfers of tithe revenue, as well as in the definition of status of the churches that received it, were quite complex. In 1217, Bishop Lawrence noted that he granted cure of souls to the four churches appropriated by the monastery of Lubiąż "by petition of the venerable Abbot Gunther of Lubiąż, on our mandate, and by request of lord James, archdeacon of Wrocław."[264] Three clerics initiated the definition of parish status: the abbot, the bishop, and the archdeacon. On this occasion, the archdeacon was also the possessor of tithe revenue from some of the localities he helped integrate into the new parishes. In 1218, Bishop Lawrence noted that the tithe from "Bartholomew's village which is now called Schönwelt," from Słup, and from Ujazd, "had belonged to lord James, archdeacon of Wrocław."[265] Tithes from another important group of villages including Dziewin, Wołów, and "the other Wołów" had been a prebend of Guido, master of the offices of the cathedral of Wrocław (magisterium Wrotizlauiense).[266]

The place-names listed here include some of the more important places documented between 1202 and 1217. Dziewin was the place where the conflict over noval tithes had been resolved about three years earlier. "Wołów and the other Wołów" was an expanding settlement between 1202 and 1217. Ujazd had been an area of settlement expansion, while between 1202 and 1218 Schönwelt was reorganized according to German law, and presumably attracted German settlers. Two places in James's tithe

---

[263]Ibid., no. 57 (1189), 33–34.
[264]Ibid., no. 157 (1217), 114.
[265]Ibid., no. 171 (1218), 124.
[266]S.U., 1: no. 171 (1218), 125. For the meaning of magisterium, see Niermeyer, p. 625, s.v. magisterium 1.

base, Ujazd and Słup, became parish centers in 1217. Thus, many of the more important sources of tithes and centers of parishes listed by Bishops Cyprian and Lawrence between 1202 and 1217 had been prebends of the cathedral clergy of Wrocław, appropriated by the monks of Lubiąż, and transferred to local churches sometime during the same period, while several of these local churches were upgraded to parochial status.

Cathedral clerics initiated and mediated transfers of tithe revenue in other ways. The canons assisted the bishop in the formal acts of transfer of tithe revenue or change of status of churches endowed with it. In 1217, Bishop Lawrence noted that he fixed the boundaries of the parishes appropriated by the monks of Lubiąż "through Guido the scholar," and explained that, on demand by the bishop, Archdeacon James, and Abbot Gunther, it was Guido who actually traced out the boundaries in his stead.[267] The role of cathedral clergy extended beyond the tracing of specifically parochial boundaries. Duke Henry once engaged the bishop and chapter to assist him in a ritual perambulation of the estate he gave the nuns of Trzebnica. Sometime between 1203 and 1208, Henry perambulated the boundary "together with lord Bishop Lawrence, with certain canons, and with my barons," and marked it out more clearly.[268]

Cathedral clerics also settled disputes over tithe revenues after their initial transfers. One dispute involved Abbot Witosław of St. Vincent's and "knight Albert," a ducal official in Wrocław. The issue was the form and timing of Albert's tithe obligations from a village in his possession. Sometime before 1228, Bishop Lawrence delegated three canons, Albert, Lambin, and Gerhard, to determine Albert's obligations. The canons were not officials of the chapter; they identified themselves as "canons of Wrocław, judges delegated by lord Lawrence the bishop."[269] They resolved the dispute without comment or other information. During the subsequent fifteen years a more complex dispute pitted the canons regular of St. Mary's and an unnamed widow of a "lord Peter" concerning possession of tithe revenue from a specified village. The widow had "unjustly occupied" the village and the tithe revenue from it.[270] The controversy was entrusted to two

---

[267]Ibid., no. 156–57 (1217), 113–14.

[268]Ibid., no. 115 (1208), 84.

[269]Ibid., no. 295 (1228), 218.

[270]Ibid., 2: no. 280 (1244), 168, lines 30–31. Nanker and Lawrence are not clear about whether the widow seized possession of the village and the tithe revenue from it, or simply the latter; they describe their mandate as "super quadam decima cuiusdam ville que vocatur Glynka, que indebite ab ipsa occupabatur."

officials of the chapter of Wrocław, Dean Nanker and Scholar
Lawrence. In 1244, they noted that they "had been delegated as
judges by lord Bishop Thomas of Wrocław" to resolve the controversy, and reported that "after some time a compromise was
reached" whereby Peter's widow was persuaded to renounce
"every right which she had believed to have with respect to the
said tithe."[271] Perhaps, by way of compromise, she was allowed
to retain possession of the village; however, Nanker and
Lawrence do not say.

In any event, the process of settling the dispute was elaborate,
and involved several third parties—including other canons of
Wrocław. The widow "fully renounced" her right to possess the
tithe "before us, the judges . . . through her worthy messengers
(*nuntii*), known to ourselves."[272] The mediators are not identified, but they were clearly persons with sustained past contact
with the chapter, and accessible to it for purposes of representing
parties to conflict in matters within episcopal jurisdiction. Their
intervention was not the end of the process of settling the dispute; "finally" (*demum*), the widow reiterated her partial retreat
"through her brother lord Berthold, son of Henry, before lord
Custodian Zdzisław and Martin, canons of Wrocław."[273] On this
occasion, the chapter of Wrocław provided judges, mediators,
and witnesses in settling the dispute. Nanker and Lawrence confirmed their document with "their seals."[274] They said nothing
about the bishop's seal or the seal of the chapter; use of seals
of individual canons once again underscores the relative importance of individual agency within the chapter as a collective group.

Cathedral canons facilitated transfer of tithe revenues at vary-
ing degrees of formality. On occasion, they acted as agents for the
clerics from outside the diocese of Wrocław with respect to transfer of tithe revenues within that diocese. Among the eight localities in Silesia whose tithes Bishop Lawrence granted to the house
of canons regular in Kamieniec in 1210, one had been a source of
tithe revenue for the dean of the Cracow cathedral.[275] The dean
alienated that tithe revenue by employing a canon of Wrocław as
his proctor. Lawrence noted that the dean of Cracow "offered as-

---

[271]Ibid., lines 31–33.
[272]Ibid., line 33.
[273]Ibid., line 34–35.
[274]Ibid., line 36.
[275]Ibid., 1: no. 122 (1210), 89.

sent" to the transfer of tithe revenue from his Silesian holding "through his proctor named Matthew, canon of Wrocław."[276] Matthew's function as proctor for his colleague from Cracow was a formal position of agency and representation.[277] Cathedral clerics in different Polish sees must have enjoyed contacts with each other, and occasionally put them to formal use in their respective ecclesiastical milieus to advance local or regional interests.

Cathedral clergy formed informal networks that ensured or at least facilitated access to bishops by clerics interested in acquisition of tithe revenue. Charters merely hint at such networks; the Henryków chronicler documents them richly.[278] Between the 1230s and the 1260s, two canons of Wrocław, Peter and Eckhard, helped the monks acquire tithe revenues in the Henryków region. Peter, provost of the chapter in the 1230s, had long been associated with the monks. On the eve of foundation of the monastery in 1222, he took part in the negotiations between Bishop Lawrence, other Polish bishops, and Duke Henry concerning the rights of patronage over the monastery.[279] Later he became an important transitional figure in the Wrocław chapter between the episcopates of Lawrence and Thomas. He was Thomas's uncle; the chronicler remembered him as "a wise man, much adorned by virtue of habit," who "ruled the episcopate in temporal matters for a few years after lord Bishop Thomas's ordination" in 1232.[280] He died in 1240.[281] During the decade preceding his death, he used the cloister as a personal retreat, visited it often to hear liturgy, and on one occasion was sufficiently impressed with Abbot Bodo's hospitality to promise him aid in procurement of additional revenues.[282]

Eckhard ascended to a position of importance in the chapter during the early years of Thomas's episcopate. This was the period of Provost Peter's dominance in the affairs of the diocese, and he might have been Peter's protégé. "Because of his great discretion," recalls the chronicler, "lord Eckhard was the highest

---

[276]Ibid.

[277]Tierney, *Foundations*, 117–27.

[278]The author was acutely aware of the significance of routine access to power, ducal and episcopal, in the maintenance of all areas of welfare and security for his monastic community; he was especially sensitive to access to the bishops of Wrocław for enhancement of tithe revenue. See Piotr Górecki,"Politics of the Legal Process in Early Medieval Poland," *Oxford Slavonic Papers*, New Series, 17 (1984): 23–44, at 31–38, 40–41.

[279]Górecki,"Politics," 33.

[280]*K.H.*, chap. 200, p. 374.

[281]Ibid., chap. 210, pp. 381–82.

[282]*K.H.*, chap. 200, p. 374.

counselor to lord Bishop Thomas in all matters, after lord Provost Peter."[283] Eckhard long outlasted Peter; he died in 1273.[284] In contrast to Peter, he never became an official of the chapter. However, his stature in the episcopal milieu far exceeded his formal position in the chapter. Throughout his tenure, he served Bishop Thomas as his proctor and negotiator in several kinds of transactions.[285] Among other things, he was involved in the uneasy relationship between Thomas and the court of Dukes Henry II the Pious and Bolesław the Bald. Sometime between 1238 and 1241, the monks of Henryków mediated one of the intermittent conflicts between the bishop and the younger Henry.[286] The bishop promised the monks a reward "for the service you provided me," and "many years later" Abbot Peter reminded the bishop of the promise, "by himself and through others familiar with him."[287] Those "others" included Eckhard, who persistently and effectively convinced the bishop to agree to a gift of tithe revenue.

The chronicler ranked the level of spiritual intercession for cathedral clerics by his community specifically according to their effectiveness in endowing the community with tithe revenue. This resulted in an exceedingly odd exclusion. Bishop Lawrence, who played an active role in the foundation of the monastery which the chronicler meticulously noted[288] is nowhere mentioned as a recipient of monastic liturgy, evidently because he compared unfavorably with Bishop Thomas as a grantor of tithe revenue. The chronicler noted a bit tartly that Lawrence "gave the cloister certain tithes out of piety, but not with the same diligence and fullness as his successor did."[289] In contrast, he effusively associated Bishop Thomas and the two canons who facilitated tithe acquisitions with the monastic liturgy. He noted that since their deaths, Canon Eckhard's and Bishop Thomas's names were repeated in the mass daily.[290] He further enjoined the monks to celebrate Thomas's death anniversary "in vigils and solemn masses forever."[291] However, the top honors went to Provost Peter; "the cloister celebrates his death anniversary by vigils, masses, and

---

[283]Ibid., chap. 205, p. 377.
[284]Ibid., chap. 211, p. 382.
[285]S.U.,3: no. 52 (1252), 46, line 1; no. 112 (1254), 82, line 33; no. 171 (1256), 119, lines 34–35; no. 375 (1261), 244, line 17.
[286]K.H., chap. 203, p. 376.
[287]Ibid., chaps. 203–04, pp. 376–77.
[288]Górecki,"Politics," 34–36.
[289]K.H., chap. 198, p. 373.
[290]Ibid., chap. 209, p. 381.
[291]Ibid., chap. 210, p. 382.

other funeral ceremonies, . . . every year and every day."[292]
The effect was a rather elaborate role of the cathedral clergy in
the process of transfer of tithe revenue over time, and an
equally elaborate network of associations of cathedral and monastic clergy.

Transfers of tithe revenues: claims, conflicts, resolutions

The contemporaries grounded the transfers of tithe revenues
between ecclesiastical possessors in precise legal language. In his
documents for the nuns of Trzebnica spanning the years 1202 and
1208, Duke Henry the Bearded was especially careful to provide
formal rationales for each of the transfers of tithe revenue from
prior possessors to the nuns. In the earliest document, written
between 1202 and 1203, he noted that the nuns acquired tithe revenue from the parish church of St. Peter's in Trzebnica "by reason
of prior right by which it was paid to St. Peter."[293] Henry must
have been pressed to explain what that "prior right" was, because later in 1203 he described himself as patron of the church,
and lord of many of the villages the church served—his formal
position towards the church of St. Peter's. He remarked that "I
gave my chapel of St. Peter with all appurtenances and all my villages established within the boundary" of the nuns' estate, and
reiterated that the nuns may receive tithe revenue "from some of
the villages by reason of the chapel of St. Peter."[294] The transfer of
tithe revenue from this portion of the estate was a straightforward appropriation of the rights of the church of St. Peter
with consent of its patron,[295] yet it required careful explanation
and record.

Henry justified transfers of tithe revenue from villages that had
not been under his lordship and that had not paid tithe to the
church of St. Peter with another formal rationale; he noted in 1202
or 1203 that tithes "from some" of the villages accrued to the
nuns "by the bishop's gift."[296] Later in 1203, he was again more
precise and explicit. He identified the bishop by his name as
Cyprian; and he described the prior lords and possessors of the

---

[292]Ibid.

[293]*S.U.*, 1: no. 83 (1202–03), 56. The relevant text is: "Decima . . . ecclesie beati Bartholomei ex integro in frugibus debetur, de quibusdam villis . . . ratione prioris iuris quo
beato Petro solvebatur, de quibusdam donatione episcopi."

[294]*S.U.*, 1: no. 115 (1208), 81, 82. Please note that this charter includes an earlier charter,
completed in 1203.

[295]Constable, *Monastic Tithes*, 61–68.

[296]*S.U.*, 1: no. 83 (1202–03), 56.

villages, and the process of transfer of possessory rights in them. "I acquired the other villages which had been ecclesiastical, or had belonged to ecclesiastics by hereditary right, or had belonged to knights, by exchange, purchase, or gift."[297] Several clerics had possessed tithe revenues from these villages. Accordingly, Bishop Cyprian's "gift" of tithes from these villages entailed compensations to the clerics who were deprived of revenue, and expressions of consent by all concerned.

These transactions resulted in rather mind-boggling sequences of exchanges and compensations. Duke Henry provided a rich sample in the first charter for the nuns. They may receive tithe revenue from the villages acquired from knights and clerics[298]

because Bishop Cyprian gave [the nuns of] St. Bartholomew the tithe from Małuszyn with the approval of Dean Benik, who had possessed it. He gave [the nuns] tithe from Raszów and part of Brochocin with the consent of Master Odo, to whose prebend it had belonged; and in place of this tithe, he gave [Odo the villages called] Kowale and Świętosz's village, which had belonged to the prebend of Bernard. And Bernard received [the village called] Skorzynice near Legnica from the bishop for these [two villages].

Elsewhere in the same charter, Henry recorded a similar chain of compensations and exchanges that was ultimately intended to benefit a canon of Wrocław named Lambert after he was deprived of the tithe revenue from another portion of the estate. Lambert's acquisition of tithe culminated several exchanges among several clerics[299]:

The . . . bishop offered the tithe of this circuit (*circuitus*) [of Kotowice] to [the nuns of] St. Bartholomew, with the consent of Lambert, the canon [of Wrocław] to whose prebend it had belonged, having given him in exchange [the tithe] from the entire village of Mienice, half [of] which had belonged to the prebend of Bernard, [and] half [of which had belonged] to [the church of] St. Peter in Trzebnica. In turn, Bernard received from Bishop Cyprian [of Wrocław] . . . [the place called] Skorzynice in [the district around] Legnica in exchange for his part of Mienice. In addition, I gave [the nuns of] St. Bartholomew the village [called] Ozorowice . . . , and since the tithe from it belonged to the parish of St. Mary in Legnica, and Bishop Cyprian, in order to give it to [the nuns of] Trzebnica, wanted to exchange [it for an area of land including]

---

[297]Ibid., no. 115 (1208), 82.
[298]Ibid., no. 83 (1202–03), 56.
[299]Ibid., 57.

as many plows (*aratra*) as there were in it, Clement, the parish priest (*plebanus*) of that church [of St. Mary in Legnica] prevailed on me with prayers [to receive tithe from the village called Chinino for it].

In addition, the Priest Clement asked the duke[300]

that I replenish the aforesaid [village of] Chinino with men [i.e., settlers], since as a result of departure of the men Clement's tithe has entirely disappeared. [Clement] declared that after this was done, he would cede the tithe from Ozorowice [to Bernard]. . . . Since I have done that as promised, Clement gratefully renounced the aforesaid tithe.

Protection of vested rights of cathedral and parish clergy to tithe revenue was an important concern during the monastic appropriation of local churches and tithes. Polish bishops had considerable authority in disposing of tithe revenue, but tithe possessors played a meaningful role in its disposal, and could expect alternative sources of support when divested of it. Most of these possessors—four of the five clerics mentioned in this charter—were cathedral canons, but the story of Clement, parish priest of St. Mary's in Legnica, shows that tithe revenue of parish priests was also protected. Bishop Cyprian had insisted to the duke that Clement and his parish church receive fair compensation for the loss of tithe revenue from Ozorowice; in addition, Clement himself asked the duke to recruit settlers into the village which was to serve as his compensation. Henry not only considered the request appropriate, but fulfilled it. The protection extended to Clement matches the general canon law rule that the primary purpose of tithes was support of livelihood of parish priests.[301]

However, despite this glimpse of protection for local clergy, that purpose seems to have disappeared from view in subsequent documents, fully in favor of attention to the cathedral chapter. Duke Henry's renewal and expansion of the charter for the nuns in 1208 refers only to possessory rights of individual canons, with no mention of Clement or any other priest.[302] In his charter for the monks of Lubiąż of 1218, Bishop Lawrence also recorded loss of tithe revenue of two canons of Wrocław, Archdeacon James and Chancellor Guido.[303]

---

[300]Ibid.
[301]Constable, *Monastic Tithes*, 85–87, 100–03, 126–28.
[302]*S.U.*, 1: no. 115 (1208), 83.
[303]Ibid., 1: no. 171 (1218), 124–25.

The relative importance of the chapter is further underscored by the fact that some parish priests were cathedral canons. For at least part of his tenure as parish priest of St. Mary's in Wleń, Henry the Bavarian held other ecclesiastical functions, including that of canon of Wrocław. In 1217, Duke Henry referred to him as "the parish priest" of Wleń.[304] In 1224, he identified him as "Henry, canon of Wrocław and chaplain of Wleń," and four years later described him as his own "chaplain" and formerly parish priest of Wleń.[305] Thus, sometime early in his career Henry the Bavarian was simultaneously canon of Wrocław and parish priest of Wleń. Between 1217 and 1228 he retired from the latter function to become a priest at Duke Henry's court. His retreat from his parochial responsibilities (whatever these were) at Wleń coincided with the appearance of the new church of St. Mary's in Bystrzyca, one of the localities within his parish.[306] It reflects the subdivision of that large parish into smaller units, and perhaps the replacement of centrally based parish clergy with a more localized cadre.

Henry's accumulation of canonical and parochial office was not unique. In 1230, Duke Henry noted a "Master Thomas, our chancellor, canon of Wrocław of the church of St. John the Evangelist, and parish priest in Oleśnica."[307] Both men held two ecclesiastical offices, and both in addition were associated with the duke's court. Nothing, of course can be said from specific cases about the frequency of accumulation of offices and benefices among the Polish clergy, or about the implication of such accumulation for performance of spiritual care. However, the pressures on their time implicit in their careers help explain the recurrent complaints of avoidance of pastoral responsibility by parish clergy and the uncontrolled proliferation of vicars.

Two cases shed light on the processes within clerical groups that effected these alienations, on the relative importance of the bishops and the clerics divested of the tithe revenue at the time of the divestment and thereafter, and on the significance of consent in the transfers. The first case concerns the canons regular of St. Mary's in Wrocław. In 1220, Victor, dean of the chapter of Wrocław, resolved a rather long-standing doubt about the quality and strength of the consent to one particular gift of tithe revenue

---

[304]Ibid., no. 164 (1217), 117.
[305]Ibid., no. 246 (1224), 179; no. 287 (1228), 211. Somewhat confusingly, Bishop Lawrence referred to him as "chaplain" of Wleń later in 1228, but may have been referring to some past time with which his document was concerned; ibid., no. 289 (1228), 212.
[306]Ibid., no. 164 (1217), 117.
[307]Ibid., no. 317 (1230), 233.

to the canons regular that had been expressed eight years earlier.[308] The doubt threatened conflict with the prior possessor of the tithe revenue, so Abbot Witosław of St. Mary's asked Dean Victor to pronounce authoritatively on the validity of the original alienation. The second case concerns the monks of Henryków. In 1233, Bishop Thomas of Wrocław deprived Nicholas, the parish priest of the settlement in and near Henryków, of the tithes from the villages granted to the monastery there, and granted the tithe revenues to the monks.[309]

The earlier problem arose as a result of an exchange of tithe revenues between a canon of Wrocław named Bogusław and the canons regular of St. Mary's. The exchange had taken place before 1212. Dean Victor recalled in 1220 that Bogusław gave up the tithe revenue from one village, and received the tithe revenue from two others[310]:

By authority of lord Lawrence, bishop of Wrocław, an exchange was effected between the house of St. Mary in Wrocław and Bogusław, canon of Wrocław, whereby the tithe from Tyniec which belonged to the said canon's prebend was ceded to the said house, while the tithe from the villages [called] Maślice and Rędzin (which had earlier belonged to that house) were ceded to the said canon's prebend.

As Victor described it, this exchange of tithe revenues had been entirely straightforward; yet it left a remarkable degree of distrust between Bogusław and the canons regular. The transaction must have been problematic right at the outset, because in 1212 both the chapter and the canons regular went to unusual lengths to record the fact that it took place. The charter in which Bishop Lawrence recorded the transaction in 1212, though unremarkable in substance, carries an unusually long witness list, consisting of the names of the canons of Wrocław. This list far exceeds any counterpart in other documents, and appears to be exhaustive.[311]

---

[308]S.U., 1: no. 198 (1220), 146–47.

[309]K.H., chaps. 65–68, pp. 264–66.

[310]S.U., 1: no. 198 (1220), 146.

[311]Beside the usual names of the bishop, some officials of the chapter, and perhaps a handful of names of other canons, this record contains a list of twenty-seven names of individual canons. As far as I know, there is no way to determine whether this unusually long list of canons was the entire chapter in 1212, because there is no independent documentation known to show the full membership at this time. At the least, however, the list of names appended to this document clearly shows extraordinary care to approximate full presence of the chapter insofar as possible. On the difficulties of establishing the full size of Polish cathedral chapters, see Zachorowski, Rozwój, 84–91; he mentions in passing that the chapter of Wrocław had 39 canons (p. 88, n. 6), but does not state the basis of that number or the time to which it refers.

It is the first extant charter to be appended by the seal of the chapter as well as of the bishop. Finally, Abbot Witosław matched the document through his own charter confirming the transfer of tithes, and in turn had it witnessed by a large group from his community.[312]

This unusual care of record directly reflects the depth of distrust among the parties involved, especially Abbot Witosław and Canon Bogusław. The distrust lingered until 1220. Victor only hinted at the causes for the distrust, but clearly stated its depth. "Since," he wrote,[313]

lord Witosław, abbot of this house, doubted the strength of the agreement because he had been told that . . . Canon Bogusław was not well disposed towards his house, and for that reason he [thought that] his consent [to the exchange] had not been very strong; and since it was also doubtful whether the charter of that exchange, which had been compiled concerning that agreement, had any force, for the reason that certain canons of Wrocław had refused to sign [it] although this charter had the seals of the bishop and the chapter [affixed to it], for these reasons, . . . Abbot [Witosław] requested anew the consent of Radulf, canon of Wrocław, who . . . held that prebend [after Bogusław], as well as the authority of the bishop and our common consent [to the exchange].

Dean Victor was in a position to know—though perhaps not tell—what went wrong in 1212; he was one of the canons present at the crowded chapter meeting that witnessed the initial alienation.[314] Abbot Witosław did not trust Bogusław's motives in entering the agreement or in abiding by it. In addition, Victor remembered serious division within the chapter about the transaction. The consent of the chapter to the transaction was not unanimous. The unusual length of the witness list of 1212 suggests that an extraordinary effort was made to compensate for that fact. This did not work. Use of seals of the bishop and chapter did not allay the resulting doubt about the finality and future

---

[312]*S.U.*, 1: no. 130 (1212), 95.

[313]*S.U.*, 1: no. 198 (1220), 146: "Sed quoniam dominus Witozlaus abbas eiusdem domus dubitabat de firmitate contractus pro eo quod dictum fuit prefatum Boguzlaum canonicum non fuisse bene prepositum domui sue ac per hoc suum non valuisse consensum, et quia revocabatur in dubium utrum aliquam firmitatem eidem commutationi carta que super ipso contractu confecta fuerat pro eo quod quidam canonicorum Wratzlauiensium negabant se subscripsisse licet eadem carta haberet episcopi et capituli sigilla, idcirco dictus abbas de novo peciit consensum Radulphi canonici Wratzlauiensis qui tunc eandem habebat prebendam nec non et auctoritatem episcopi et nostrum communem consensum."

[314]*S.U.*, 1: no. 129 (1212), 94.

reliability of the agreement. Nor did time. Canon Bogusław, the butt of Witosław's distrust, was succeeded by Radulf, yet Abbot Witosław wanted to resolve his concern by a definitive solution. His concerns show that, between 1212 and 1220, a division within the chapter over a transfer of tithe revenues resulted in a cloud on the alienation despite formal expressions of corporate consent. Witosław's fears show the relative importance of meaningful consent by the individual canons for the security and finality of the alienation; in this respect, the conflict confirms other impressions of the importance of the individual canons within their corporate group.

Abbot Witosław asked for a new expression of consent to the exchange by Bogusław's successor, by the bishop, and by the chapter. However, he got much more. Victor decreed that[315]

when the bishop says that he gives his authority to this [type of exchange] because of a work of piety, it is not only permitted by law to make such an exchange with the said canon to the prejudice of his successor, but also to diminish this prebend, as long as [the resulting] prebend is adequate [to support the successor].

In addition to the remedies Abbot Witosław asked for, Dean Victor confirmed for the bishop and the possessor of a prebend broad authority to alienate tithe revenues at the expense of existing prebends and their future possessors. Unfortunately, Victor articulated the rule impersonally and in the passive voice, and did not expressly state which member of the cathedral clergy had the right to make the initial alienation. In the context of the controversy, however, his statements that "it is permitted . . . to make such an exchange with a canon to the prejudice of his successor," and "to diminish this prebend" must mean that the initial party to the agreement was the canon alienating the revenue. Thus, Canon Bogusław had had the capacity to enter into the exchange with the monks during the original transaction.

This capacity depended on three further conditions: consent by the bishop; a motive of "piety" in making the grant; and adequate revenue of the diminished prebend to support the successor of the alienating cleric. Victor did not list consent by the chapter, or by the canons other than the grantor of the revenue, among the

---

[315]Ibid., no. 198 (1220), 146–47: "Nos autem videntes de iure posse non tantum commutationem fieri cum predicto canonico in preiudicium successoris eius, sed etiam mutillationem eiusdem prebende cum prebenda esset sufficiens cum idem episcopus diceret propter opus pietatis in hoc suam prestitisse auctoritatem."

conditions validating the initial alienation. His omission is puz-
zling in view of the difficulties posed by the ambiguities in the
canons' consent to the initial exchange. It also seems inconsistent
with the contemporary stress among European canon lawyers on
consent by the chapter in transactions concerning the endowments of the chapter.[316]

Despite the silence, Victor did not consider the consent of the
chapter dispensable. On the contrary, he himself consented to
the initial exchange and to its renewal in the presence of the
Wrocław cathedral chapter. "We have tendered our consent in order that this exchange remain strong forever."[317] The document
closes with the witness list, prefaced with the information that
the confirmation took place "in the presence of Victor the dean,
John the archdeacon, Guido the scholar, Lawrence the custodian,
Guido the chancellor, and many other canons and vicars and clerics of this church."[318] Thus, consent of the chapter remained important, but only after the other essential preconditions were
fulfilled. These preconditions involved only the alienating cleric
and the bishop. Thus, Victor described the terms of the initial
alienation whose fulfillment should have deprived the canons of
any grounds for objection, and presumably disposed of the objections the canons expressed to the initial exchange.

The rule articulated by Victor strengthened the legal position of
the bishop towards the chapter by clarification of those rights of
the bishop and the alienating cleric which would elicit the chapter's consent, perhaps as a matter of course. The later story, culminating in 1233, shows a parallel enhancement of the bishop's
role in monastic appropriation of the tithe revenues of parish
priests. The story begins in the years before the endowment and
the foundation of the Cistercian monastery in Henryków, that is,
before 1222.[319] Among the many inhabitants of the area included

---

[316]On this subject, see in general Tierney, *Foundations*. Tierney implies that throughout
medieval Europe the years 1200–20 were a relatively early period in the definition by
canon lawyers of the corporation as a legal entity, of the corporate rights of the chapter,
and of prebends as corporate property of the chapter. The conflict resolved by Victor is
therefore best seen as one of what must have been an enormous number of individual
conflicts between bishop, chapter, and individual clerics, to which the canon lawyers were
responding with the corporate theory described by Tierney while the conflicts were underway.

[317]*S.U.*, 1: no. 198 (1220), 147.

[318]Ibid.

[319]For the timing and process of the endowment in 1222, see Górecki, "Politics," 31–39;
for the earlier background of the participants, see Zofia Kozłowska-Budkowa, "Przyczynki do krytyki dokumentów śląskich z pierwszej połowy XIII wieku" [Contributions to
source criticism of the Silesian documents from the first half of the thirteenth century], in
Studia z historii społecznej i gospodarczej poświęcone Franciszkowi Bujakowi (Lwów, 1931), pp.

in the monastic estate since 1222 were two brothers, Stephen and Nicholas. They owned one of the villages later included in the estate, Skalice; in addition, Nicholas was parish priest of Henryków and the surrounding area of settlement. The chronicler noted that "Nicholas was a priest and the legitimate rector of the church of Old Henryków."[320] The chronicler said nothing explicit about the way in which Nicholas became priest. He noted that prior to the monks' arrival in 1227 "Nicholas the . . . rector of Henryków received tithes throughout the entire district of Henryków . . . out of the arable of lord Nicholas, then patron of the inheritance."[321] Bishop Thomas added in 1261 that Nicholas had been supported by tithes from a total of six named villages within the estate of Henryków.[322] The latter Nicholas arrived in the region in the first decade of the thirteenth century, acquired several holdings, and consolidated them into a single estate.[323] The tithe from that estate supported the priest, his namesake. This sequence of events suggests that the church staffed by Nicholas the priest was part of the estate of Nicholas the patron, and that the latter recruited the former to furnish cure of souls for the population of the expanding estate. The two Nicholases constitute another story of parish formation in areas of expanding arable, settlement, and lordship.

Nor did the chronicler explicitly state when and by whom the parish church was established. Before 1228, a "wooden church" had existed in Henryków, and in that year was adapted as the first cloister church for the newly arrived monks by consecration of two additional altars.[324] If this was indeed Nicholas's parish church, this step did not necessarily terminate its parochial status. It presumably crowded the liturgy a bit, but displaced neither the faithful from the church nor their priest from his function. The accounts of Nicholas's spiritual role in Henryków and vicinity after arrival of the Cistercians lapse into obscurity. In a passage describing events subsequent to the year 1233, the chronicler described him as "the cloister's own chaplain" (*proprius capellanus*

1–6; for the local rural society affected by the formation, see Heinrich Grüger, "Das Volkstum der Bevölkerung in den Dörfern des Zisterzienserklosters Heinrichau im mittelschlesichen Vorgebirgslande vom 13–15. Jahrhunderts," *Zeitschrift für Ostforschung*, 27 (1977): 241–61; and Górecki,"*Viator* to *ascriptitius*: Rural Economy, Lordship, and the Origins of Serfdom in Medieval Poland," *Slavic Review*, 42 (1983): 14–35, at 19–26.

[320] *K.H.*, chap. 65, p. 264.

[321] Ibid.

[322] Ibid. In 1262, Kołaczów was a substantial territory, including four named villages.

[323] Górecki,"Legal Process," 32–33; idem, "*Viator* to *ascriptitius*," 21–25.

[324] *K.H.*, chap. 21, p. 249.

claustri).[325] At the time the chronicler wrote, Bishop Thomas of Wrocław also remembered Nicholas as "chaplain" of "the brothers" in Henryków, and noted that tithe revenue from several specified villages included in the estate of the monks "had once been given to the parish church" there.[326]

As these clerics recalled later, Nicholas's exact position underwent a transformation; the monks appropriated the endowment of his parish church and presumably the church itself while he became the monks' "own chaplain." The term *capellanus proprius* resembles a common expression for a parish priest, *sacerdos proprius*.[327] Thus he may have retained his role as parish priest under new patronage; but this is precisely the issue on which the documents are most obscure. The chronicler, in any case, noted that Bishop Thomas accused Nicholas of idleness. Thus, after 1228 his spiritual role in the locality either in fact diminished or became vulnerable to political pressure. In either case, his position under monastic patronage became ambiguous and uncomfortable.

Meanwhile, on the eve of the monks' arrival in 1227, the prebend of the parish church supported the rector comfortably. "This church in Henryków" noted the chronicler, "flourished with great revenues at that time."[328] The expansion of revenue corresponds to the period when the other Nicholas was consolidating the individual holdings into a single estate (*campus*). After the monks arrived, the prebend became even more lucrative, and so was Nicholas's tithe revenue. Perhaps embarrassed with the resulting riches, Nicholas gave his portion of the village of Skalice to the monks. The chronicler noted that[329]

for a few years after the arrival of the convent, he received this tithe from the cloister's plows. Since, as a result, he received enough [revenue] after the arrival of the brothers, and thought that he would always receive the tithe from the cloister's plows for himself, he said to his brother Stephen, "I see that thanks to the arrival of the . . . brothers . . . my prebend has quite increased, so I wish to assign the part of the inheritance [of Skalice] which belongs to me to the cloister in perpetual possession." . . . A few days later, this Nicholas came up to . . .

---

[325]Ibid., chap. 68, p. 265.

[326]*S.U.*, 3: no. 448 (1263), 295, lines 15–17, 27–29.

[327]Morris, *Papal Monarchy*, 536; Avril, "Paroisses et dépendances monastiques," 102–03; idem, "A propos du *proprius sacerdos*: quelques réflexions sur les pouvoir du prêtre de paroisse," in *Proceedings of the Fifth International Congress of Medieval Canon Law* (Vatican City, 1980), 471–86.

[328]*K.H.*, chap. 65, p. 264.

[329]Ibid., chaps. 65–67, pp. 264–65.

Duke [Henry I] . . . and before him granted [his portion of] Skalice to
this cloister to be possessed forever. . . . This gift was made before Duke
Henry . . . in the year of the Lord 1233.

Nicholas's actions show his expectations concerning his possession of tithe from what had been his parish, and his reaction to
these expectations. Despite appropriation of the parish by the
monks, Nicholas retained possession of tithe revenue. The chronicler implies that Nicholas granted his portion of Skalice in order
to compensate the monks for his windfall enrichment caused by
the establishment of the monastic estate within his parish. Thus,
he expected to continue receiving tithe revenues from the prebend in the future. His continued possession of the tithe revenues
is consistent with the protection extended to tithe possessors
against monastic—specifically Cistercian—appropriation of tithe
revenues by the Fourth Lateran Council in 1215. That protection
was effective as of 1233.

   However, Nicholas was soon disappointed. The events that followed his gift to the monks show the limits of the conciliar protection of ecclesiastical tithe possessors in the face of Cistercian
estate expansion and appropriation, and the role of Bishop
Thomas—fondly remembered by the monks later—in establishing those limits. Merely "a few days after" Nicholas made his ill-
considered gift, Thomas visited the cloister with his retinue.
"Upon noting," refers the chronicler,[330]

that the brothers who lived there were in the most acute poverty, he
asked lord Henry, abbot at that time, and the brothers about the cloister's revenues and . . . wealth. When he heard from the abbot and the
brothers that the cloister's plows were paying tithe to . . . Chaplain
[Nicholas], the lord bishop became very angry, summoned this Nicholas, chaplain of Henryków, before himself, and told him, "You sit here
by yourself and do nothing but sing with the sparrows! I want these
brothers to receive the tithe from this part of the village [of] Henryków
for themselves."

Nicholas was deeply disturbed for the next two years. "When he
heard the [bishop's words], Chaplain Nicholas was distressed by
a great sadness of mind, but did not answer anything right
there."[331] In raising the possibility of protest, the chronicler implies that it was conceivable for Nicholas to object, but that an

---

[330]Ibid., chap. 68, p. 265.
[331]Ibid.

objection would have been of no use. Nicholas's rather meek posture seems quite different from the response by Clement, the parish priest of Legnica, who had successfully sought compensation for the tithe revenue appropriated by the nuns of Trzebnica thirty years earlier. The contrast in responses by the two priests suggests that the relative role of the bishop in the appropriation of tithe revenues had increased at the expense of the parish priest in the preceding three decades or so. Bishop Thomas surely thought so in his later commentary on the appropriation of Nicholas's prebend. In a record of the tithes granted to the Henryków monastery, he noted that Nicholas had possessed the tithe revenue from the monks' estate "by the grace of our predecessor [Bishop Lawrence] and of ourselves."[332] In putting it this way, he construed Nicholas's possessory right in the tithe revenue very narrowly.

Nicholas somehow managed to hold on to his prebend for another two years. It seems that even Bishop Thomas's aggressive insistence on the full appropriation did not lead to immediate results, but instead opened a fairly long period during which the appropriation was completed. What happened in that period is not clear, but Nicholas finally left to become a canon regular at a nearby Augustinian house, and Bishop Thomas granted the lucrative revenue from his prebend to the monks[333]:

Two years afterwards, [Nicholas] resigned the chapel of Henryków into the abbot's hands, and transferred himself to [the house of] the order of the [canons] regular in Kamieniec. From that hour and time the large income of the chapel of the village of Henryków was removed by the venerable lord Thomas, bishop of Wrocław, and given to the cloister.

Nicholas's story shows some of the options available to a cleric whose prebend revenue was undergoing appropriation as of the third decade of the thirteenth century. The impending deprivation of his prebend revenue was distressing and inconvenient, but Nicholas was not entirely without remedy. Although at the beginning of the thirteenth century Clement insisted on compensation for the tithe revenue Bishop Cyprian assigned to the nuns, in 1233 Nicholas kept unhappily quiet, and stayed put for two additional years until he secured an opening at a monastic establishment nearby. That house had been endowed continuously

---

[332]*S.U.*, 3: no. 448 (1263), 295, lines 27–28.
[333]*K.H.*, chap. 68, pp. 265–66.

since 1210.[334] Its existence gave Nicholas an option for compensation that Clement did not have around 1200. It must have made Bishop Thomas's intervention more palatable to Nicholas than Bishop Cyprian's had been to Clement.

The cases of Priest Clement, of Canons Bogusław and Radulf, and of Priest Nicholas suggest a change in the relations within the groups of ecclesiastics concerned with the alienations. The decisions of Dean Victor and of Bishop Thomas appear to reflect a shift in the balance of rules in the transfer of tithe revenues between the bishop and both categories of present possessor (that is, cathedral canon and parish priest) in favor of the bishop. Thus, during the first three decades of the thirteenth century, effective control over the tithe revenues of an appropriated parish slipped from the hands of the parish priest who had possessed the revenues prior to the appropriation. On the other hand, opportunity for compensating a parish priest in this position increased during the same period. The availability of the house of the canons regular at Kamieniec may have encouraged Nicholas to wait out the two difficult years without major protest. Thus, the thickening network of ecclesiastical institutions and endowments in this region sharpened hierarchical authority within the network, and at the same time enhanced the participants' options for adjusting to that authority.

---

[334]*S.U.*, 1: no. 122 (1210), 88–89, no. 152 (1216), 110, no. 316 (1230), 232–33; see; Silnicki, *Dzieje*, 372–73.

4. TITHE PAYMENTS AND CATEGORIES OF POPULATION: OBLIGATION AND PRIVILEGE

Status and tithe obligations in the early thirteenth century

Twelfth-century sources are even less eloquent about tithe obligations of specific categories of people in the Polish duchies than they are about the churches supported by tithe revenues. In his short narrative about the unnamed "certain noble" who founded a church, Gallus said nothing about revenues for the church, tithe or other. Pope Innocent's bull of 1136 records the content of tithes and the castellanies from which tithes were due, but does not impose these tithe obligations either on specific localities within each castellany, or on specific inhabitants or categories of inhabitants. The twelfth-century records of endowment of the canons regular of St. Mary's and St. Vincent's in Wrocław impose tithe obligations on specified localities, but similarly do not associate these obligations with any persons or personal status.[335] Quite possibly, in the earlier twelfth century, tithes were not levied directly on the population at all, but deducted from revenues gathered into the castellanies or other places.[336] The earliest record of subjection of specified localities to tithes is the group of documents recording the endowment of the houses of Augustinian canons regular in Wrocław. If so, then the twelfth century was a pioneering period in the establishment of a system of tithe obligations for different categories of inhabitants in the archdiocese of Gniezno.

Whenever that system originated, its earliest record is the documentation of attempts at its reform by Bishop Lawrence after 1207, and the resulting twenty-year conflict with Duke Henry. The documentation of that conflict records the tithe obligations—and of exemptions from tithe—of different categories of inhabitants of the duchy of Silesia before and after the conflict. The documents refer to long usage; they reflect an established and

---

[335]S.U., 1: no. 19 (1139–49), 15; 23 (1149–50), 18.

[336]If Modzelewski is right, the tithes described in 1136 were a tenth of royal revenues brought into each *castrum*; see *Organizacja*, chap. 1.

traditional pattern of tithe obligations and exemptions, and an established and traditional social structure. They describe some of
these obligations and exemptions as specific to the archdiocese of
Gniezno, and so generalize them to the Polish duchies in the entirety. Several of these distinct features of the Polish tithing system occupied the attention of Polish bishops and papal legates
concerned with the archdiocese of Gniezno later in the thirteenth
century. The resulting evidence sheds light on the structure of
the economy and society in the Polish duchies, the differentiation of status among their inhabitants, and on the regional role
of the institutional Church in affecting and accommodating
these contexts.

In their compromise of 1227, the judges delegate noted that the
bishop had demanded canonical tithes from several categories of
the duke's subjects, and that the duke and bishop reached a distinct compromise about the tithe obligations of each category of
inhabitants. As a result, the judges' record is rather complicated.
They categorized the inhabitants according to several criteria: territory, status, ethnicity, and land use. They grouped the duchy of
Silesia into basic territorial districts, "castellanies," and defined
the tithe obligations of the inhabitants of each castellany according to the other criteria.[337] They divided the province into two
groups of castellanies. The inhabitants of the first group were
subjected only to the tithes they had been paying before 1226, regardless of their status. "The bishop promised that he would
henceforth not request other tithes from the castellanies of
Krosno, Bytom, Żagań, Bolesławiec, and Wleń beside those
which the people (*homines*) of these castellanies were in the habit
of paying until now."[338] The inhabitants of the second group of
castellanies were subjected to an altogether different tithing
régime. In the castellanies of Goścień and Otmuchów, "wherever the forest is being settled (*ubicumque silva locata fuerit*), a
quarter-mark shall be due from each hide; except for every sixth
hide . . . which shall accrue to the pioneering settler (*locator*)"
free of tithe.[339]

Beneath these general clauses, the judges described tithe obligations of the inhabitants of the two groups of castellanies at different levels of detail. Inhabitants of the first group of castellanies
were a diverse population, and were subjected to a correspond-
ingly diverse range of tithe obligations. Inhabitants of the castellany of Krosno were categorized according to ethnicity. The duke

---

[337]Kuhn, "Kastellaneigrentzen," 12–13.
[338]*S.U.*, 1: no. 281 (1227), 207.
[339]Ibid.

and bishop subjected Germans to three measures of grain from each hide of arable, "while," as the judges put it, "the Poles shall pay as they have paid until now."[340] Inhabitants of the castellany of Bytom were classified according to status, ethnicity, and implicitly geographic mobility and recent resettlement. "The men of the duke (*homines ducis*) shall pay the tithe in honey, as they have paid until now. The free [peasants] (*liberi*) and the Jews, wherever they plow [land], shall pay the tithe in its entirety (*ex integro*)."[341] Inhabitants of the castellanies of Żagań and Bolesławiec were not categorized according to any criteria; they were all subjected to a tithe in honey, similar to that imposed on "the duke's men" in the castellany of Bytom.[342] Inhabitants of the castellany of Wleń were subjected to tithe in squirrel skins, likewise without distinction of status, ethnicity, or economic specialization.[343] Finally, inhabitants of the region between Goścień and Otmuchów were not categorized by any of the criteria used to classify the inhabitants of the first. The sole distinction among them was the privileged position of the *locator*.

Despite—or perhaps because of—the differences of emphasis, assessment, and detail within and between these two records, the judges delegate give us a skeletal structure of the economic differentiation of the recorded regions of the duchy of Silesia, and of the relationship of that differentiation to status and ethnicity. The principal source of tithes in grain around the turn of the century included the Germans settled in the castellany of Krosno, the free peasants (*liberi*), and Jews settled in the castellany of Bytom; the principal source of tithes in honey included the "men of the duke" settled in the castellany of Bytom, and everyone living in the castellanies of Żagań and Bolesławiec. The principal source of tithes in squirrel skins were inhabitants of the castellany of Wleń. The principal source of tithes in coin were the new settlers of the forests in the castellanies of Goścień and Otmuchów. The obligation of Poles settled in the castellany of Krosno to "pay as they have paid until now" is uncertain.

This list of tithe obligations does not approach the full spectrum of economic specializations or statuses in the Polish duchies in the first decades of the thirteenth century; it should emphatically not be used to resuscitate old stereotypes of a vaguely pre-agricultural essence of the early Slavic or Polish economy and

---

[340]Ibid. For treatment specifically of German settlement in that castellany over a much longer time span, see Kuhn, "Kastellaneigrentzen," 13–35.

[341]Ibid.; see Kuhn, "Kastellaneigrentzen," 39–44, emphasizing German settlement.

[342]Ibid.

[343]Ibid.

society. We know from obligations other than tithes that inhabitants of the Polish duchies frequently specialized in a broad range
of output in conjunction with agriculture, and that they were
subjected to obligations across that broad range, in different
combinations.[344] Subjection of inhabitants to tithes in, say, squirrel skins or honey may indeed mean an intensive specialization
in hunting or beekeeping, but in view of the purpose of the document it may mean the exact opposite; namely, that these activities were relatively unimportant, and that Lawrence's attempt to
tithe other areas of rural specialization was at the root of the conflict with Henry.

We have a bit of independent information on the range of resources subject to tithe within one of the castellanies recorded in
1227, the castellany of Wleń. In 1217, Bishop Lawrence recorded
the content of tithe revenues due to the parish church at Wleń
from several villages within that castellany. According to the
compromise of 1227, inhabitants of that castellany were obliged to
pay tithe in squirrel skins. Ten years earlier, the bishop noted
that ever since its consecration in the mid-twelfth century, the
parish church at Wleń had indeed received tithe in squirrel skins
from one village, but that sometime after the turn of the century
the content of that tithe was changed to grain. "Whereas squirrel
skins (*asperioli*) had previously been given as tithe to [the church
from] Bystrzyca, the aforesaid princes [Duke Henry the Bearded
and his wife, Duchess Hedwig] have changed them into a grain
tax (*annona*)."[345] The shift towards agricultural produce was not
complete; the tithes for St. Mary's in Bystrzyca included a mix of
other products, obtainable from the forest which bordered on the
three villages included in the tithed area. Henry and Hedwig
"also [granted] the tithe . . . from the honey from this side of the
forest. . . . To that [they added] the tithe from marten skins (*mar-
duribus*) from this side of the forest, and six marks."[346] The sum of
six marks due from the forest was substantial, and indicates that
the forest remained an important local source of economic resources despite the shift towards agriculture within the full range
of tithed products. Who exploited this forested perimeter, and
how, are entirely unclear.[347]

---

[344]Górecki, *Economy*, 76–101, 243–55.

[345]*S.U.*, 1: no. 164 (1217), 117.

[346]Ibid.

[347]It seems to have been exploited by, or under the supervision of, a relatively few specialized laborers or officials; the forest tithes in honey, skins, and coin were placed on two
persons settled in the forest, and rather mysteriously referred to as *centuriones*. Their status is entirely unclear from this document, and they do not appear elsewhere; in the con-

The content of the tithe revenues in the castellany of Wleń recorded in 1217 partly overlaps with the content of the tithe revenues from all the castellanies listed in the compromise of ten years later. Taken together, the documents of 1217 and 1227 show, in rather different ways, the areas of the social output which the duke and bishop—from different vantage points, and for different reasons—considered the most worthwhile subjects of tithe. The two documents also suggest the basis and the economic significance of the compromise of 1227. In 1227, Bishop Lawrence allowed the inhabitants of the castellany of Wleń to pay tithe in squirrel skins, as they had traditionally done, thus restoring the tithing régime that had existed in at least one village of that castellany since the mid-twelfth century, and that had only recently been changed. What happened to the rest of the obligations Lawrence had listed in 1217? Perhaps the judges delegate simply left them unrecorded; they were, after all, dealing with tithe obligations at the level of castellanies, not the individual villages that made them up, and may have referred to squirrel skins as shorthand for the essential obligations of the castellany of Wleń taken as a unit, in conscious disregard of local variation.

But in view of the nature of the conflict, I would guess that the tithes in grain, honey, marten skins, and coin recorded in 1217 had been among the bishop's new demands that irritated the duke and provoked the conflict. Between 1207 and 1217, these products must have become increasingly important in the rural economy, while squirrel skins were becoming marginal. The bishop attempted to subject all of them to tithe, but by 1227 was compelled to give up the attempt, and return to the traditional payment. Thus, the relationship of the list of tithe obligations compiled in 1227 to the dynamics of economic specialization in the duchy is quite complex and subtle. That list constitutes merely an initial and rather rough guide to the range of economic specializations within parts of the duchy of Silesia. However, it does not always record the most dynamic or important sectors within that range. On the contrary, it occasionally and for good reason reflects those areas of specialization and production that were relatively traditional and peripheral. To that extent, it underrates the fluidity, diversity, and dynamism of economic and demographic change.

---

text of the locality with which Lawrence deals, they seem to have been ducal forest wardens, each in charge of managing, or at least collecting tithes from, the specified resources. (Ibid.) Beyond this information, the *centuriones* are somewhat enigmatic; most scholars consider them to have been heads of large groups of the ducal slave *decimi*, organized into hundreds. See Karol Buczek, "O chłopach w Polsce piastowskiej" [The peasants in Piast Poland], part 1, *Roczniki Historyczne*, 40 (1974): 50–105, at 58, 66–68.

In some other respects, however, the record of 1227 does suggest a relative importance of several regions, specializations, and populations within the duchy. Perhaps the most striking general feature of the record is the contrast between the two groups of castellanies, and the populations in each group. Despite all their diversity of status, specialization, and geographic mobility, the inhabitants of the castellanies of Krosno, Bytom, Żagań, Bolesławiec, and Wleń were subjected solely to their traditional tithes. As of 1227, these five castellanies were therefore a region of existing and articulated settlement. In contrast, the region between "the boundaries of Goścień and Otmuchów" was essentially a destination for new clearing and immigration. Both regions attracted new settlers. Of the two, the latter was, relatively speaking, a frontier of settlement and lordship.[348]

The immigrants were largely German settlers. In 1217, Pope Honorius referred specifically to Germans as parties to the controversy between the duke and bishop. In a letter to Henry, he noted "the controversy which has arisen between you and our venerable brother, the bishop [of Wrocław] concerning the tithes owed by certain Germans, who have newly (*de novo*) been recruited to live into this land."[349] Thus, by 1217 German immigration into the diocese of Wrocław had been substantial; the Germans were the category of peasants most sharply specialized in agricultural clearing and production; and they were the shrillest and most systematic opponents of the tithes claimed from such lands by the bishop. How unique were the Germans in these respects? Lawrence's reference to the "free peasants" and the Jews, "wherever they plow land," suggests that these other categories of settlers were geographically mobile; but the relative emphasis of the documentation indicates that of the geographically mobile categories of inhabitants of the duchy of Silesia in the early thirteenth century, the Germans were the most conspicuous.

The tithe obligations for the inhabitants of the regions between Goścień and Otmuchów spelled out in 1227 correspond exactly to terms of settlement of German immigrants in Silesia formulated throughout the 1220s. Clearing arable, its division into hides (*mansi*), and the privileged role of the *locator*—the pioneering

---

[348]Otmuchów was a center of a castellany in the region of the river Nysa, where the bishops of Wrocław established a major estate of the diocese; the early phases of the expansion of that estate took place in the 1220s. See Walter Kuhn, *Siedlungsgeschichte Oberschlesiens* (Würzburg, 1954), 41–44; Silnicki, *Dzieje*, 152–54.

[349]*S.U.*, 1: no. 153 (1217), 111.

German settler who recruited other peasants into new settlements—all recur as standard terms in contemporary plans for settlement of German immigrants, or perhaps of other settlers "according to German law." At the height of their conflict, Henry and Lawrence formulated plans for tenures of two German pioneering settlers that contained tithe exemptions matching the compromise of 1227. Both recipients were expected to recruit new settlers into the places granted to them, to expand their present arable or its forested periphery, to divide them into hides, and to retain special rights in the specified proportions of the hides. In 1221, Duke Henry wrote that[350]

we gave Menold the village called Budzów, to be established (*locari*) out of fifty hides [of uninhabited land, in exchange] for [every] sixth hide, which shall be free from the payment of all tax and tithe. And if something [i.e., some area of additional forest] should exceed the fifty hides of forest, we join it to the said village according to the same law.

Two years later, Bishop Lawrence provided that a pioneering settler named Walter was[351]

to settle (*locare*) Germans in the territory (*territorium*) of [the Wrocław episcopal church] St. John in Ujazd, [in exchange] for every sixth hide . . . , whose tax and tithe this Walter shall receive with his heirs, free and quit in perpetuity, for his expenses and labors in the foundation and rule of the said place.

Whatever their other disagreements, the duke and the bishop shared an interest in this particular tenurial modification of canonical tithe obligations, and the judges delegate left it intact specifically in those regions of the diocese of Wrocław where further expansion through recruitment of German peasants was anticipated. This compromise was yet another confirmation of the existing tithing practices in the duchy at the time of the conflict.

On balance, the compromise of 1227 appears to represent a victory by Duke Henry in the conflict against the bishop. However, Lawrence did not suffer total defeat. He managed to impose tithes on several categories of inhabitants who had been exempt from tithes altogether. The terms of their subjection to tithe payments in 1227 offer a glimpse into the patterns of marginality, importance, and privilege within the society under the twin power

---

[350]Ibid., no. 210 (1221), 154–54.
[351]Ibid., 1: no. 225 (1223), 164. Please note that this is not the Ujazd in which Bishop Lawrence established a parish under the patronage of the monks of Lubiąż in 1217.

of duke and bishop. These categories of inhabitants were quite distinct from the rest of the population and from each other. They are listed apart from the castellanies that served the judges as a grid in describing everyone else; and they were settled under sharply articulated ducal lordship. Pope Honorius noted in his 1226 mandate to the judges delegate that Bishop Lawrence had sought tithe payments from a ducal servile group[352]:

Whereas the predecessors of the said Bishop [Lawrence] have completely relaxed the tithes of certain slaves (*servi*) of this duke commonly called the *smardi*, and received several of his slaves of this condition, together with certain possessions, in compensation for the tithes [due] from them, the said Bishop [Lawrence] nevertheless requires and extorts tithes from them against justice.

Duke Henry gave way on the bishop's demands from this and several other groups. "Since," the judges delegate wrote in 1227,[353]

by the abuse of a crooked custom (*prava consuetudo*) and by a certain antiquity [of practice] the men (*homines*) commonly called the *smardones*, the *lazaky*, the guards (*strozones*), the *popraznici*, [and] the plowmen (*aratores*) did not pay tithes, the said duke obliged them . . . to a full payment of tithes for the good of the peace (*pro bono pacis*).

The documents shed very uneven and scarce light on the meaning of these categories of inhabitants. Honorius clearly referred to the *smardones* as unfree.[354] Like serfs and slaves elsewhere in medieval Europe, they were not exempt from tithing by virtue of their unfree status, and had on one recent occasion been subject to monastic tithes.[355] The legal status of the other three groups

---

[352]Ibid., no. 261 (1226), 191.

[353]Ibid., no. 281 (1227), 207.

[354]Little else is known about the group. Compare Kazimierz Tymieniecki, *Smardowie polscy: studium z dziejów społeczno-gospodarczych wczesnego średniowiecza* [The Polish Smards: a study in the socioeconomic history of the early Middle Ages] (Poznań, 1959), with Buczek, "O chłopach," pt. 1, pp. 83–95. For divergent views of other, sparsely documented groups indicated in the documents, called the *stróże, poprażniki,* and *łazęki,* compare Kazimierz Tymieniecki, "Łazęki," *Słownik Starożytności Słowiańskich*, 3 (Wrocław, 1967): 113–14, and the cited literature, with Buczek, "O chłopach," pt. 1, pp. 95–98.

[355]Constable, *Monastic Tithes*, 32. In this passage, Constable notes that "[e]ven slaves . . . must pay tithes," according to one Carolingian council. He offers this evidence as part of his exposition of the biblical and canonical theory of tithe liability (ibid., 13–16, 31–35, 198), and not of the practice of tithe gathering from different categories of the population (including the free, serfs, and slaves). He does not squarely reach the question of how the theory was implemented; however, by expressing surprise that "even slaves" were subject to this obligation, he implies that the practical operation of that formally universal obligation was uncertain, and that the populations subjected to it varied. This is more than implicit in his extensive discussions throughout the book of the impact of lordship, infeudation, property law, and inheritance law on the control over, content of, and

cannot be ascertained.[356] Whatever the precise meaning of their individual statuses, Duke Henry's willingness to subject them and solely them to the full tithes demanded by the bishop suggests that he saw them as economically the least important population in the duchy.

Another category of inhabitants that had traditionally been exempt from tithe were knights (*milites*). Their tithe obligations after 1227 represent only a partial concession by Henry. The duke "compelled those of his knights who obtained, or may yet obtain, villages worthy of tithe payments from the duke since the [Fourth] Lateran Council to pay the tithes they owe by law, but according to knightly law, that is, they may give tithes . . . according to their will" to the churches of their choice, "with damage to other churches."[357] Lawrence succeeded in subjecting this category of inhabitants to tithe, but with two important qualifications. Only knights who had settled in Silesia recently, or who were to settle there in the future, were to be subject to tithes and even they were allowed an unusual degree of choice in the performance of the obligation. Knights who had been settled in the duchy prior to 1215 continued to be exempt from tithes altogether. For them, the compromise was yet another retreat by the bishop; but regarding their successors, the bishop was now armed with the canons of the ecumenical council, and that was clearly worth something.

It was worth the knightly privilege; part of that privilege consisted of the right to grant tithe revenue to a church chosen by the grantor. Polish prelates grudgingly accepted the privilege, and focused their efforts on controlling its abuse, though with escalating impatience about the privilege itself. In 1223, Bishop Lawrence noted tithe revenues "freely granted by certain knights" to a monastery in Rybnik, and recorded the grant "so that the church of the Holy Savior . . . not be defrauded in any way."[358] His ecclesiastical superior took a similar though a bit more severe position on this privilege in the provincial council of 1233. After observing that "through tolerance or concession, the

---

possession of tithes. In a bull issued in 1193 to confirm and protect the endowment of St. Mary's monastery in Wrocław, Pope Celestine III included a reference to a group of "*smardones* with their tithes." *S.U.*,1: no. 61 (1193), 39.

[356]Their economic specializations are at least suggested by the etymology of their status terms. The *strozones* should have been settlers specializing in some guarding role. The *popraznici* and the *lazaky* appear to have been mobile groups specializing in clearing forests for cultivation; the root of the first name has been associated with burning, and of the second with traveling to inaccessible places. For the meaning of *stróża*, see Górecki, *Economy*, 147, 150.

[357]*S.U.*, 1: no. 281 (1227), 207.

[358]Ibid., no. 226 (1223), 165.

church of Poland has allowed the knights of Poland to pay tithes to churches of their choice," Archbishop Pełka accused the knights of not paying tithes in full, and threatened such knights with loss of "this right which is allowed to knights," so that as a result "they shall pay as do those who do not have the privilege of knighthood (*privilegium militie*)."[359]

The knights' ability to assign tithes from their villages to ecclesiastical recipients of their choice was a defining feature of knightly status.[360] The documents of 1223, 1227, and 1233 did not question the privilege, but merely sought to compel the knights to turn over the proceeds to the church of their choice. The position of knighthood in the duchy was thus both privileged and ambivalent. Knights were clearly one of the groups newly settling in the duchy on favorable terms. They must have bitterly resented the imposition of any tithe, and successfully resisted imposition of retroactive tithe. Those who were subjected to tithe obtained an unusual role in its disposition. However, Pełka's threat of loss of knightly status indicates that knights could potentially be threatened with downward mobility by prelates using canonical jurisdiction to enforce provisions of canon law. That potential increased in the course of the thirteenth century.

Compromise and conflict: "knightly law" and Polish knighthood in the thirteenth century

The contrast between the remedies of 1227 and 1233 suggests that in the decades following the ecumenical council of 1215 leading ecclesiastics were becoming increasingly strict in enforcing local tithing arrangements in a manner favorable to ecclesiastical possessors. The trend towards strictness continued

---

[359]Ibid., 2: no. 34 (1233), 21, lines 33–38.

[360]Knightly status consisted of several other areas of privilege and honor, which underwent substantial change during the later twelfth, thirteenth, and fourteenth centuries. Control over tithe revenue was one of these areas of privilege. The pioneering work on this status is Zygmunt Wojciechowski, *Prawo rycerskie w Polsce przed statutami Kazimierza Wielkiego* [The knightly law in Poland prior to the statutes of Casimir the Great] (Poznań, 1928); the post-war Polish historians have contributed several major studies situating prosopographic analysis of Polish knighthood in a broad context of economy, politics, and lordship. See above all Cetwiński, *Rycerstwo*; Cetwiński, *Rycerstwo śląskie do XIII wieku: biogramy i rodowody* [Silesian knighthood through the end of the thirteenth century: biograms and genealogies] (Wrocław, 1982); Janusz Bieniak, "Rody rycerskie jako czynnik struktury społecznej w Polsce XIII–XIV wieku (Uwagi problemowe)" [Knightly kindreds as a factor of the social structure in Poland in the thirteenth and fourteenth centuries: Remarks on the issues], in Henryk Łowmiański (ed.), *Polska w okresie rozdrobnienia feudalnego* [Poland in the period of feudal fragmentation] (Wrocław, 1973), 161–200.

in subsequent years, when bishops and legates began to invalidate the "privilege of knighthood" itself by denying secular landholders the choice of ecclesiastical recipient of tithe revenue altogether.

In 1234, Bishop Thomas issued a document in which he denied any future possessors of eleven Polish villages the right to assign tithes from them to any church beside their current ecclesiastical possessor[361]:

Because . . . these villages have been subject to payment [of tithe] since long ago, we establish that their heirs, of whatever condition they should be, shall pay the tithe to the [ecclesiastical recipient] in the entirety, as they do at present, forever and devotedly. And it shall not be licit for anyone [else] to receive it [i.e., the tithe revenue] to the prejudice of [that ecclesiastical recipient].

The bishop approved of payment of tithes by the heirs of the village to the intended beneficiary "in the entirety, as they do at present." Thus, he was not concerned with any abuses in the process of the payment, and did not question any past grant of tithe revenue from these villages to the ecclesiastical institution. He was concerned solely with the heirs' future ability to grant that tithe revenue to an ecclesiastical institution other than its current possessor. He also denied that choice to any future possessors of the villages. Tithes from this group of villages were permanently to accrue to their present recipient. Legate Guido generalized this protection of current tithe possessors in 1267; he provided that once tithe revenue has been granted, no layman "shall by his own will or rather presumption grant [tithes] to anyone else, [to any] church or person; but whoever used to receive the tithes from a place, shall [continue] to receive them without contradiction."[362] Thomas and Guido did not refer to the lay possessors specifically as knights, or to the choice of church as "knightly." However, the choice they sought to terminate was the defining element of the "privilege of knighthood."

The wide choice of Polish knights in disposing of tithe revenues from their villages led to another problem of ecclesiastical control. The knights recurrently treated these tithes as a part of their inheritance, and sought to restrain their alienation. In 1248,

---

[361]*S.U.*, 2: no. 60 (1234), 38, lines 34–37.
[362]*K.Wp.*, no. 423 (1267), 373.

Legate James described knightly opposition to sales of the tithes
they controlled, and sought to eliminate that limitation on their
acquisition by ecclesiastical institutions. He directed a statute[363]

[a]gainst knights who impede the sale of tithes. We consider this intolerable,
that certain knights . . . seeking to keep the tithes of their own or of another's villages, interfere in various ways in order to prevent any of the
religious men [i.e., monks, canons, or priests] from buying them. . . .
And so the tithes of the churches disappear and the ecclesiastical rights
are diminished. And sometimes it happens that when a knight opposes
[a sale of] a tithe [over which he has had control] for many years, his
heirs say that the [proceeds of the tithe] belong to them by hereditary
right.

In contrast to the writers of 1227 and 1233, the legate did not approve of these practices, but threatened their perpetrators with
ecclesiastical censure and mandated the Polish prelates to carry
this out. Nevertheless, restraints on alienation of tithe revenues
remained problematic for the next twenty years. Legate Guido returned to this practice in his 1267 statute, and provided for alienability of tithe revenues. He decreed that present recipients of
tithe revenues[364]

may sell the tithes delivered to them by the peasants as seems advan-
tageous to the convenience of themselves and [their] churches. Any layman . . . who secretly or openly presumes to impede this kind of sale,
should understand that he is prohibited from entering a church until he
makes amends for such a fault in a worthy manner.

In contrast to James, Guido did not specify who the present recipients of the tithe revenues were. Whereas James had clearly
indicated that the tithes in question were due from knightly villages, and identified knights as the group that placed restraints
on the sales of tithes, Guido appears to have been concerned with
sales of tithe revenues by any possessor, and with restraints on
alienation by "any layman." Guido's norm was phrased more

---

[363]S.U., 2: no. 346 (1248), 204–16, at 207, lines 40–47: "Contra milites qui impediunt ven-
ditionem decimarum. Illud autem precipue intollerabile reputamus, quod quidam milites
vel alii clerici vel laici volentes villarum suarum vel aliarum decimas obtinere diversis mo-
dis impediunt ne aliquis a viris ecclesiasticis eas emat, ut decimas ipsas inivitis illis ad
quod pertinet occupare valeant violenter, et quandoque promittunt se reddituros pro illis
minus in duplo vel triplo quam valeant, et tamen vix aut nunquam volunt etiam ea solvere
que promittunt. Et sic pereunt ecclesiarum decime ac iura ecclesiastica minuuntur. Et interdum contingit quod cum aliquis miles sic decimam aliquam renuerit multis annis, here-
des eius decimas illas dicunt ad se iure hereditario pertinere."
[364]K.Wp., no. 423 (1267), 373.

broadly than James's; it subsumed James's earlier specific concern with actions by knights under a general protection of alienability of tithe revenues by anyone from lay interference.

In addition to these problems of control over tithe revenues, knights sometimes reduced or dismissed altogether the tithe obligations of the peasants they recruited into their villages. The problem dates back at least to the turn of the thirteenth century, when Duke Henry I was recruiting knights into Silesia in substantial numbers. Bishops and papal legates addressed it in the documents of 1233, 1248, and 1267. In his synodal legislation of 1233, Archbishop Pełka provided that people settled under knightly lordship should pay their entire tithe. "We direct that all [people], of whatever condition they should be, shall pay the tithe in the entirety . . . , even though they are the plowmen of the knights (*licet sint aratores militum*)."[365] Fifteen years later, Legate James associated this difficulty specifically with German knights who had been settling in the Polish duchies and recruiting German peasants to settle under their lordship. He issued a statute entitled [*A decree*] *that the knights may not relax the tithes of the peasants*, and continued[366]:

It sometimes happens in these parts [i.e., Polish duchies] that some duke or prince wishing to retain German or other knights in his service concedes to them in fief (*in feudum*) some lands situated within his lordship (*dominium*), from which [lands] the settlers (*coloni*) of some church or of some ecclesiastical person had been paying a proper tithe (*rectam decimam*) from of old. These knights, wishing to be generous to another [peasantry] in order to receive a larger rent from the aforesaid lands, settle [the lands] with other peasants (*agricolae*); and out of the aforesaid

---

[365]*S.U.*, 2: no. 34 (1233), 21, lines 32–33: "Item precipimus quod omnes cuiuscumque sint conditionis decimam ex integro persolvant . . . licet sint aratores militum." Perhaps the estates of the knights referred to in this rather obscure passage were what Hoffmann, following several Polish and German scholars, calls "demesne farms"; see Hoffmann, *Land, Liberties, and Lordship*, 94–104, 427. If I follow Hoffmann correctly, "demesne farms" include all estates whose arable has not been subject to division and rent according to German law.

[366]*S.U.*, 2: no. 346 (1248), 208, lines 1–12: "Ut milites colonis decimas non remittant. . . . Contingit enim interdum in partibus istis quod aliquis dux vel princeps volens milites Teutonicos vel alios in suo servitio retinere concedit eis in feudum terras aliquas in suo dominio constitutas, de quibus coloni alicui ecclesie vel persone ecclesiastice consueverunt rectam decimam solvere ab antiquo. Illi vero milites volentes de alieno facere largitatem ut maiorem censum de terris recipiant antedictis, aliis agricolis locant eas quibus remittunt de terris predictis sextum mansum omnino a decima liberum et sextam partem aliarum omnium decimarum promittentes eisdem, quod ipsos de eadem remissione erga omnes clericos liberabunt. Unde contingit quod si forte episcopus vel alia persona ecclesiastica que de eisdem terris rectam consueverunt decimam recipere, dictos agricolas super hoc inquietant, dicti milites per minas et occupationem bonorum suorum illos compellunt ut ab huiusmodi inquietatione desistant."

lands, they allow [the new peasants every] sixth hide to be entirely free from tithe, and allow them to retain a sixth part of all the other tithes, and promise them that they will free them from this payment to all clerics [altogether]. As a result it happens that if a bishop, or another ecclesiastical person who has been accustomed to receive a proper tithe (*rectam decimam*) from these lands, should by chance disturb the said [newly settled] peasants (*agricolae*) about this [in order to claim their rightful tithe], the said knights compel [the ecclesiastical tithe claimants] to desist from this disturbance by threats and by occupation of [their] goods (*occupatio bonorum*).

This clause briefly reconstructs the recruitment of German knights and peasants into the Polish duchies, and the impact of the resulting immigration on tithe revenues and on control over tithe collection. "Dukes and princes" recruited German knights, sought "to retain them in service," and gave them lands "in fief" for this purpose. James's description of 1248 matches the reference by the papal judges delegate in 1227 to Polish knights whom Duke Henry I had been establishing in Silesia around 1215. The judges delegate had not referred to the Polish knightly tenures as fiefs or as "feudal," and had not even implicitly associated these tenures with service to the duke. Between them, the documents of 1227 and 1248 show a deliberate ducal policy of recruiting knights and establishing knightly tenures, and a uniform adaptation of the Western language of fiefs as a formal expression of these tenures. Immigration of German knights was the specific occasion for the use of that language.

In turn, the knights, "German and other," recruited German settlers into Polish territories. The settlers moved into areas previously inhabited by other, presumably Polish, peasants (*coloni*). The earlier peasants had paid "proper tithes" to ecclesiastical tithe possessors; the tithes were gathered "in the field." The exemption from tithe of every sixth hide of the land resettled with Germans sharply altered the tithing practices to which the Polish inhabitants of these territories had been subjected, and changed the balance of revenues from the farms. Whereas rent payments to the knights increased, tithe revenues to ecclesiastics fell.

The exemption of a sixth of the arable from tithe had been a standard term of settlement by Germans in the Polish duchies since at least the 1220s. For all their disagreements, Duke Henry I and Bishop Lawrence of Wrocław included this term in their charters for pioneering German settlers, and the papal judges delegate had approved the exemption for the arable of the *loca-*

tores to be recruited into several peripheral regions of the duchy of Silesia in the tithe schedule of 1227. However, in 1248 the exemption was controversial, and James disapproved of it, or at least portrayed it as a problem. Why the difference in response? It seems that between 1227 and 1248 the primary economic purpose of the exemption changed. According to the earlier documents, the primary aim of the exemption was to attract German settlers to peripheral areas of previously existing Polish villages and of the duchy as a whole. Both duke and bishop welcomed the exemption as a recruitment device. By 1248, the primary aim of the exemption was to attract German settlers to move under knightly lordship and protection into areas where a Polish peasantry had been settled earlier.

The resulting pattern of lordship substantially interfered with the tithe possessors' traditional access to tithe revenues. When ecclesiastics approached the German peasants to collect the traditional tithe revenues from the arable, the knights routinely seized parts of their estates in order to deter the tithe claims. In addition, the knights sought to bar ecclesiastical tithe possessors from the field altogether. "The aforesaid knights," James continued,[367]

also do something else which very much aggravates the said deed[s]: they refuse to pay even the amount they owe beyond the said sixth hide and the sixth part of all tithes in the field, as has been customary to do, but [instead want to pay it] in their barn[s]. And they pay a certain number of measures [of grain] far smaller than the proper amount (*rectus numerus*) of the tithes. And so sometimes all the right which God had in the tithes [from these lands] disappears.

German knights must have prevented ecclesiastical tithe possessors from sending their tithe collectors (*decimatores*) into the lords' or knights' fields at harvest time, and measuring out of the tithe before the grain was removed to the lords' or knights' barns, threshed, and stocked.[368] The measurement of tithes now took place at the end, not the beginning, of the harvest. Thus, ecclesiastical tithe possessors lost control of the initial measurement of

---

[367]*S.U.*, 2: no. 346 (1248), 208, lines 12–17: "Faciunt etiam milites antedicti aliud quod valde aggravat dictum factum: nam etiam illud quod deberent solvere ultra dictum sextum mansum et sextam partem omnium decimarum, in campo nolunt persolvere secundum quod fieri consuevit, sed in horreo suo. Et non decimas vel nomine decime, sed quendam solvunt numerum mensurarum longe minorem recto numero decimarum, ut sic aliquando omne ius quod deus habet in decimis deleatur."

[368]For the *decimatores* see Constable, *Monastic Tithes*, 131–32.

the grain available for tithing.[369] As a result, the knights seized part of the tithe they owed to the possessors. Among other things, this practice undercut the priority of tithe payments over all the other charges on the land that had been enunciated at the Fourth Lateran Council and widely followed by the Polish tithe debtors thereafter.

This problem of control over the disposition of tithe revenues by German knights paralleled the difficulties posed to ecclesiastical tithe possessors by Polish knights. Archbishop Pełka had noted in 1233 that Polish knights controlled the collection of tithes in the fields in their villages, and that they often seized part of the tithe revenue they gathered as a result. Control by German knights over tithe revenues from German peasants entailed a different process, but posed analogous difficulties. The conflict over the place of tithe collection was an attempt by Polish and German knights to seize control over measurement of grain, the key commodity in which rents from Polish and German peasants were due by the mid-thirteenth century.[370]

Throughout the first half of the thirteenth century, the knights had been victorious in this conflict, and the ecclesiastical tithe possessors had been in retreat. The result of the conflict was a sharp definition of knighthood in the Polish duchies in terms of control over the collection and disposition of grain tithes from peasants. The peasantries whose grains were thus controlled, and the specific patterns of the control differed; the peasant statuses, tenures, and payments differed; and perhaps the Polish and German knighthoods otherwise differed.[371] Overarching these differences, however, was a sharp distinction between all knights and all peasants implicit in an analogous pattern of control.

Legates James and Guido sought to remedy these results. James provided that[372]

---

[369]The timing of gathering tithes with respect to the harvest varied in other regions of Europe; see Boyd, *Tithes and Parishes*, 198–205.

[370]For competition over control of grain measures in early modern Poland (set in rich comparative perspective), and its implications for social stratification, see Witold Kula, *Measures and Men*, tr. by R. Szreter (Princeton, 1986), 47–50, 55–57, 59–61, 62–63, 130–46, 148–55. In contrast to Kula, I do not think that this conflict was in any sense a class struggle. It did not pit lords against peasants; it pitted knights against ecclesiastics. It was a struggle between different categories of lords.

[371]For an attempt at a comparison of German and Polish peasants, see Górecki, *Economy*, 249–55; note the very different approach by Hoffmann, *Land, Liberties, and Lordship*, 81–82.

[372]*S.U.*, 2: no. 346 (1248), 208, lines 17–23: "Quia igitur ex predictis et deus et homines offenduntur, ea tolerari de cetero prohibemus nisi forte urgens necessitas vel evidens utilitas hoc requirat, vobis, qua fungimur auctoritate, mandantes ut omni personarum accep-

[s]ince . . . God and men are offended by the aforesaid [deeds], we prohibit them to be tolerated in the future, unless by chance an urgent necessity or an evident utility should require it. We mandate you [the
archbishop and bishops] . . . to restrain the aforesaid knights from the
aforesaid excesses, without exception for any person, and to compel
[them] to make satisfaction for [deeds] committed in this way, so that
their fault (*culpa*) does not begin to be your own. Nor shall you permit
[tithed land] to be withdrawn from the proper payment (*solutio recta*),
and [from the collection of payment in] the usual place, and [from pay-
ment] as tithes. [You shall carry out this mandate] in order that through
carelessness you do not neglect to preserve what had been acquired
by your predecessors by much sweat and—if this is right to say—by
much blood.

James's remedies were rather circumspect. He severely directed
the archbishop of Gniezno and his suffragans to reverse the state
of affairs which led to the loss of ecclesiastical revenue, but did
not spell out any particular remedy which the prelates could use
for that purpose. Remarkably, the sole sanction he spelled out
was directed at the bishops themselves; he implied that if they
permitted the loss of tithe income to ecclesiastical tithe possessors to continue, they would be held responsible for the loss. In
addition, he allowed the controverted knightly practices in case
of "urgent necessity or great utility." He did not explain the exception, but placed the burden of establishing its scope and ap-
plicability, and of devising the sanction, on the Polish episcopate.
He did not threaten the offending knights with any punishment.
On the face of it, his reform was therefore quite limited.

Not surprisingly, the problem continued during the subsequent decades. In 1267, Legate Guido dealt forcefully and explicitly with all the problems James had addressed in 1248. "If," he
wrote,[373]

[laymen] give their lands to others to be cultivated [in tenure], they shall
not presume to absolve them [i.e., the tenants] from payment of tithes,

---

tione [sic] exclusa prefatos milites a predictis excessibus compescatis et ad satisfaciendum
de commissis taliter compellatis, quod culpa eorum non incipiat esse vestra, nec sustin-
eatis ut recedatur a solutione recta et loco consueto et nomine decimarum, ne quod per
multos sudores et, si fas est dicere, sanguines est a vestris predecessoribus acquisitum,
conservare per incuriam negligastis."

[373]*K.Wp.*, no. 423 (1267), 373: "Si vero terras suas aliis tradiderunt colendas eos nec in
toto nec in parte a solucione decimarum presumant absolvere, cum non sit iustum ut ea
que Dei sunt et ministrorum ecclesie personis conferant alienis, sed tam de sexto manso
quam de omnibus partibus aliis ipsi coloni decimas integraliter persolvere non omittant.
Alioquin tam ipsos colonos quam defensores seu fautores eorum ab hac presumpcione
que furtum vel rapina non immerito dici potest per denegacionem ecclesiastice sepulture
et subtractionem Sacramentorum ecclesiasticorum precipimus coherceri."

in full or in part, since it is unjust for those [things] which belong to God and to servants of the Church to be granted to other persons. The peasants shall not neglect to pay these tithes in their entirety, from the sixth hide as well as from all the other parts [of the arable]. Otherwise, we direct that the peasants themselves, as well as their protectors or patrons (*defensores seu fautores*), be restrained from this presumption which may justly be called theft or plunder by a denial of ecclesiastical burial and by a withholding of the sacraments.

James passed problems onto Polish bishops; Guido resolved them. First, he prohibited tenurial modification of canonical tithe obligations, specifically the exemption of every sixth hide from tithe that was characteristic of German tenures. Thereby he formally ended one of the special tithing arrangements on which Duke Henry and Bishop Lawrence had agreed before 1227. Second, instead of chastising and threatening the Polish episcopate, he enforced the prohibitions with precise sanctions, directed squarely at the peasants and the laymen who recruited them and protected them from rightful claims by tithe possessors. As in his other statutes, he did not explicitly identify the peasants' "protectors" as knights, but the provision must have been directed at the knights. He made no exceptions to the prohibition.

Guido's statutes culminated a long process of escalation of ecclesiastical sanction against local arrangements regarding control over and payment of tithes. Bishop Lawrence initiated the process sometime between 1207 and 1217 by demanding canonical tithes from a wide variety of categories of inhabitants. The resulting conflict ended in compromise, which substantially confirmed the diversity of tithe obligations and control over the gathering and disposal of tithe. In particular, the compromise affirmed the distinct rights towards gathering and disposal of tithe revenues that defined the Polish "privilege of knighthood." Archbishop Pełka confirmed that privilege in 1233. Over the subsequent half-century, Polish and German knights continued to settle in the duchy, and intensified knightly control over tithe revenues. Ecclesiastical response gradually shifted from grudging acceptance in the 1227 and 1233, through exhortations to Polish bishops to do something in 1248, to express prohibitions on essential aspects of knightly control over tithes in 1267.

The practical impact of these gradually escalating remedies cannot be assessed. At the very least, the problems these remedies addressed, and the change in these remedies over time, trace out several transitions in the structure of the Polish society and economy. The responses by bishops, legates, and papal judges delegate were carefully tailored to the constraints posed by complex social processes, and the parties at whom the responses were addressed were allowed considerable scope for their practical resolution. The remedies presume that the basic social and political processes that gave rise to the grievances could be stopped with great difficulty if at all, and aimed at their authoritative accommodation and at a control of some of their results. They reflect a clear emergence of knighthood in the Polish duchies ever since the anonymous court chronicler of Bolesław the Wrymouth sketched out the role of "a certain noble" in ecclesiastical formation and endowment a century and a half earlier.

Compromise and conflict: level and timing of tithe obligations in the thirteenth century

At first glance, the image conveyed by the ecclesiastical authors of the conflicts between clergy and knighthood may seem an almost Manichean struggle of good and evil. Of course, this impression is utterly misleading. On their side, ecclesiastical tithe possessors recurrently engaged in a practice to enhance their tithe revenues illicitly. They delayed the gathering of tithe from the fields after the harvest in order to extort from peasants a level of tithe payment beyond their canonical obligation. In the title of a statute of the 1248 synod, Legate James stipulated "that those to whom tithes are owed should receive them within eight days after the harvests,"[374] and described the nature of the abuse. He noted that[375]

some [tithe possessors] . . . refuse to receive the tithes which are offered to them and which the tithe debtors are prepared to pay them immediately after the harvests have been completed, even after they are urgently requested [to receive the tithes] by the [tithe] debtors. They

---

[374]*S.U.*, 2: no. 346 (1248), 204–16, at 207, line 26.

[375]Ibid., lines 31–39: "quidam contra legem huiusmodi venientes decimas que eis debentur et que debitores completis messibus eis statim solvere sunt parati, nolunt recipere etiam a debitoribus instantius requisiti, volentes eos per hoc cogere ad ipsas decimas quantum voluerint comparandas. Nam cum de consuetudine patrie debitores decimarum non possint suas novem partes removere de agro nisi prius decima persoluta, si pro ipsis decimis tantum dare noluerint debitores quantum requiritur ab eisdem, illi, quibus debentur, hac consuetudine abutentes decimam suam in agro scienter corrumpi potius patiuntur, ut et novem partes debitoris decime in agro pariter corrumpantur." (The *lex* to which James refers at the beginning of the cited portion of the canon is natural law, which he uses as a source of his condemnation of the abuse.)

wish thereby to compel them to furnish [them with] tithes in the amount which they wish [to receive in addition to the canonical tenth]. And since according to the custom of the country the tithe debtors may not remove their nine parts [of the grain] from the field unless the tithe has been paid first, if the debtors refuse to give the tithes in the amount in which they are demanded of them, those to whom the tithes are owed abuse that custom, and knowingly suffer their own tithe to be destroyed [instead of accepting the tithe revenues as soon as they are offered to them], so that the debtor's nine parts [of the grain] in the field are destroyed equally [with the grain owed as tithe but not received]. . . . Henceforth, we prohibit the inflicting of this abuse, and mandate that you are to act in the matter of receiving your tithes so that the poor [i.e., the peasant tithe debtors] are not aggrieved.

The practices that enabled the abuse, and the abuse itself, illustrate the process of tithing in the Polish duchies around the mid-thirteenth century. The tithes were customarily paid in grain. James was entirely unconcerned with any other tithes. It does not follow that the diversity of tithe payments stipulated by the compromise of 1227 was discontinued, but does show an increase in the relative importance of grain within that diversity in the subsequent two decades. James's emphasis confirms the intensification of the agricultural dimension of the rural economy during the previous first half of the thirteenth century.

In the absence of the abuse, tithe revenues were collected "in the field," as soon as possible after the grain was harvested. Presumably, the grain was arranged into shocks and left in the fields, where ecclesiastical tithe owners sent out their estate agents. The agents designated the appropriate proportion of the shocks to be removed into the owners' "farms" or barns, and threshed there.[376] Tithe payments had priority over all other charges on the proceeds from the land. This rule of priority had been clearly articulated at the Fourth Lateran Council.[377] By the mid-century, it was routinely accepted in the Polish duchies. The tithe debtors from whom the tithes were demanded were eager to turn over the tithe to the agents at once, in order to gather the grain needed for other purposes and obligations. James recognized that this rule of priority was followed "according to the custom of the country." The conflict therefore was not engendered by local re-

---

[376]Legate James did not elaborate on the exact process of how the tithe was gathered in the fields. For details of how tithes were gathered, see: Boyd, *Tithes and Parishes*, 198–207, at 205; Constable, *Monastic Tithes*, 131–32; Modzelewski, *Organizacja*, chap. 1; Jerzy Kłoczowski, *Europa słowiańska w XIV–XV wieku* [Slavic Europe in the fourteenth and fifteenth century.] (Warsaw, 1984), 84.

[377]Mansi, vol. 22, col. 1042D-E, chapter 54.

sistance to an ecumenical canonical rule, but on the contrary by its widespread acceptance.

After entering the fields, the collectors held off the gathering of the tithe in order to coerce the tithe debtors to pay a level of tithe higher than was canonically due. The ultimate sanction of this demand was destruction of the entire crop (tithe and all) by allowing it to rot in the field. In response, Legate James fixed the number of days within which the tithe possessors were obliged to collect the tithes, and commanded the Polish bishops to enforce that time limit against the ecclesiastical tithe possessors who were committing the abuse.[378]

The abuse continued in the subsequent decades. Legate Guido returned to the problem in 1267. Like James, Guido did not question the basic practices which were abused; on the contrary, he affirmed them. At the outset, he approved of the practice of tithe payment "in the field." "We strictly admonish," he wrote, "that tithes shall be paid in the field. It shall not be proper for any layman, noble or ignoble, of whatever power or dignity he should be, to dare to infringe boldly upon the said custom."[379] He coupled this confirmation of a customary practice with a detailed prohibition of its abuse[380]:

Since we want laymen to be obedient concerning the collection of tithes, we wish to relieve them of a burden which is said to be [brought against them] by ecclesiastical persons concerning delay or hindrance in the gathering of tithes. We establish by the present decree that without regard to any [other] arrangement, regulation, or agreement after the crops are gathered in the field, a triple announcement shall be made to him to whom the tithes are owed, under suitable witness and at appropriate interval (each of which should last at least two days), so that he can remove his tithe, [and] so that the peasants do not suffer damage to

[378]*S.U.*,2: no. 346 (1248), at 207, lines 26, 35–39.

[379]*K.Wp.*, no. 423 (1267), 370–75, at 373: "precipimus ut iuxta laudabilem consuetudinem patrie decime in agro persolvantur; nec liceat alicui laico nobili vel ignobili, cuiuscunque dignitatis vel principatus existat, consuetudinem memoratam propria temeritate infringere."

[380]Ibid.: "Verum sicut laicos circa preceptum de decimis persolvendis esse volumus obedientes, sic eos a gravamine ecclesiasticarum personarum quod eis inferre dicuntur super dilacione vel mora percipiendi decimas relevare volentes, presenti decreto statuimus ut non obstante aliqua constitucione, ordinacione seu composicione, postquam segetes in agro collecte fuerint, ei cui decime debentur sub testimonio competenti et per intervalla congrua quorum quodlibet ad minus duos dies continget, trina fiat denunciacio ut decimam suam tollat, ne propter eius dilacionem vel moram ipsi coloni in suis novem partibus sustineant detrimentum. Alioquin elapso triduo a tempore denunciacionis ultimo facte, novem partes suas libere ipsis liceat ubi voluerint collocare. Nos enim sentencias excommunicacionis vel interdicti quas hac occasione fieri contingerit in colonos decernimus irritas and inanes."

their nine parts because of his delay or hindrance. Otherwise, after
three days have passed from the final announcement, they [i.e., the
peasants] may freely gather their nine parts [to] where[ever] they wish.
And we declare any sentences of excommunication or interdict pro-
nounced against the peasants in this matter null and void.

Guido's narrative outlines the conflicts and their consequences in
detail. First, the abuse was perpetrated specifically by ecclesiastics against laymen. Second, it was clearly routine and familiar as
of 1267. Guido referred to it generally as a "delay or hindrance in
the gathering of tithes," without spelling it out as James had
done in 1248. Third, the laymen responded by "disobedience" to
the tithe demands made under these circumstances. Guido did
not explain the meaning of that "disobedience," or who among
the laymen was expressing it. It was in any event a substantial
threat to ecclesiastical revenues. Other clauses suggest the forms
it took. Guido's strong affirmation of tithe payment "in the field"
suggests that tithe debtors sought to move the place of the payment out of the field into barns or other stocking places, where
the threat of delay would not place the entire crop in jeopardy. In
addition, Guido forbade commutation of customary tithe obligations to cash payments. "Under penalty of excommunication,
we . . . prohibit prelates or other ecclesiastical persons from presuming to change the payment of tithes so commendably observed in this province to a cash payment."[381] Perhaps one of the
motives for commutation was to deny ecclesiastical tithe possessors their customary access to the peasant grain "in the field."
Guido confirmed both of the traditional tithing practices, and
thus sought to secure the possessors' traditional access to tithe
revenues. At the same time, he sought to end the practices which
led to resistance to that traditional access. The intended effect
therefore was to strengthen the traditional privilege of Polish ecclesiastical tithe possessors.

Meanwhile, the ecclesiastical tithe possessors responded to the
"disobedience" by excommunicating peasants. Peasants were
therefore specifically aggrieved by the abuse (as James had implied), and active in resisting it. Guido voided this sanction. He
also provided a fixed period of time within which the tithe possessors retained priority in receiving the tithes over other charges
on the crops, and spelled out a set of actions which the peasants

---

[381]Ibid.: "Addicientes et sub pena excommunicacionis prohibentes ne aliqui prelati vel
ecclesiastice persone solucionem decimarum, in hac provincia tam laudabiliter obser-
vatam, commutare presumant in pecuniariam pensionem."

and tithe possessors were to perform within this period of time. The peasants were to inform the tithe possessors that the tithe was ready to be gathered from the field. Notification by peasants as such was not new; twenty years earlier, Legate James had noted that peasants routinely informed tithe possessors that their tithes were available, and urged them to gather the canonical tenth from the field. However, Guido formalized that notification into a series of steps whose performance placed an obligation on the tithe possessors to gather their tithes promptly, and excused the peasants from following the priority rule if the possessors failed to do so. The steps for notification were fairly elaborate. The notification was to be manifest; it was to be repeated up to three times, with substantial intervals between the repetitions. The total time planned for notification was at least six days after the harvest. In addition, the tithe possessor had an additional five days since the third notification to gather his tithe. He lost priority in gathering tithes only after that time.

Thus, Guido placed a limit of at least eleven days on the possessors' right to gather his tithes prior to all other claimants after the harvest. He apparently considered the limit adequate to prevent the damage James had complained about. However, Guido's limit was considerably longer than James's limit of eight days since the harvest. During the intervening twenty years, the standard of adequacy must have shifted adversely to the peasants. Perhaps for good measure, Guido made the practice uniform, and voided all local, specific solutions to this problem. Thus, as finally articulated, the reform was quite generous to ecclesiastical tithe possessors. It represents yet another case of accommodation of regional practices while mitigating some of their harshest results.

CONCLUSION

The German prelates delegated by Honorius III in 1226 to me-
diate the conflict between Bishop Lawrence and Duke Henry confronted a social and political scene that was complex and in sharp
transition. The solutions of the conflict embodied in their document of 1227 accommodated that complexity and transition, and
legitimated much of the controversial practices by both bishop
and duke. The specific controversies to which they responded occupied ecclesiastics in subsequent generations. Thus, the conflict
spanning the years 1207 and 1227 offers insight into social, legal,
demographic, and economic continuity and change in the duchy
of Silesia, and situates the history of the institutional Church
within that context.

The conflict between Lawrence and Henry concerned, among
other things, demographic expansion. The late twelfth century
and the first decades of the thirteenth were a period of expansion
of settlement, arable, and population. Population grew both
through immigration of settlers from outside the duchy or region
within it, and through more local subdivision of relatively old
localities. The process cut across divisions of status; as the
Henryków chronicler put it later—perhaps with deliberate vague-
ness—the dukes recruited "the noble and the mediocre" continuously at least since the mid-twelfth century, and settled them
in regions in which they sought to expand and consolidate
authority.[382] "The noble and the mediocre" included knights (*milites*) and several categories of peasants. The process also cut
across divisions of ethnicity. The knights recruited were both
Polish and German, a distinction clearly recognized by contemporaries. On the other hand, the peasants are unevenly documented; Germans are the most conspicuous category of peasants
recruited into and within Silesia, but there is considerable evidence of recruitment, migration, and resettlement by Poles.

Expansion of population implied expansion of arable, intensification of agriculture, expansion of regional centers of exchange,
authority, and cult (that is, towns), and definition of lordship.

---

[382]*K.H.*, chaps. 2–3, pp. 238–39; chap. 82, p. 276; chap. 113, p. 299.

These interrelated processes affected, among other things, tithe obligations of various categories of inhabitants of the duchy, and resulted in a wide variety of obligation, exemption, and control over tithe revenue. Each of several categories of inhabitants was subjected to tithe obligations that were either assessed differently, or collected differently, depending on ethnicity, formal status, and region of settlement. Recent settlers and the lords who recruited them claimed exemption from noval tithes. One category of inhabitants was either exempted from tithe payments altogether, or granted the right to donate tithe revenues to a church of their choice. They were the "knights"; this free choice was a defining element of the "privilege of knighthood" (*privilegium militiae*), which the judges delegate and their reforming successors recognized as specific to the archdiocese of Gniezno. The privilege allowed its beneficiaries control over revenues of particular churches, and meant a close dependence of churches on the laity. Secular landholders controlled local churches in other ways; in particular, they were important in establishing local churches, and routinely possessed parish churches, a fact papal legates and Polish bishops considered a distinctive characteristic of the archdiocese of Gniezno. They helped select the clergy that staffed these churches, and faced bitter opposition from popes and prelates in this respect.

Another category of inhabitants exempted from payment of tithe were German immigrants who assumed responsibilities for recruiting new German settlers into particular localities possessed by dukes or other lords. By the middle of the century, a variety of people availed themselves of the "privilege of knighthood," while the pioneering German settlers took on other knightly attributes.[383] Exemptions from tithe contributed to a definition of uniform privilege for social groups somewhere within the chronicler's amorphous cohort of the "noble and mediocre," and help explain what he meant by that expression.

Tithe obligations reflected other economic processes and areas of social differentiation. Change in the content of tithes reflected an intensification of the agricultural sector of the economy in the course of the thirteenth century. After 1207 Bishop Lawrence had attempted to shift the content of tithe obligations towards grain, but failed; as a result twenty years later the papal judges delegate restored payments in a wide gamut of products, ranging from squirrel skins through honey to grain. But by the time Legate

---

[383]Górecki, *Economy*, 238–40, 257, 266.

James reflected on the same society in 1248, he clearly assumed that tithe obligations of Polish as well as German peasants were routinely due in grain, that they were customary, and that there was a preferred mode of gathering of tithe "in the field," identified expressly as yet another practice specific to the archdiocese and a "Polish custom."

The society on which James and his successor Guido commented in 1248 and 1267 was intensively tithed; the subject of the ensuing grievances was physical control over the actual grain from which the tithe was to be gathered. Ecclesiastical tithe possessors and the knights from whose holdings tithes were due struggled bitterly over the specific location in which the grain was to be measured out. German knights in particular insisted that the grain be moved from the field to barn before it was actually measured out, while tithe possessors sought to have access to the entire crop before it was moved anywhere from the field. On their side, those ecclesiastical tithe possessors who retained access to the grain "in the field" pressured peasants and their lords to pay them at a level that exceeded the canonical tithe obligation level by refusing to gather the rightful tithe immediately after the harvest, and threatening the entire crop with destruction in the field. The Polish and Italian prelates considered these pressures by knights and ecclesiastics specific to the archdiocese. They deplored them in general, but partially accommodated them in practical detail. The result was a structure of ecclesiastical and secular privilege within a dynamic demographic and economic setting.

Although knights and dukes frequently possessed tithe revenues, the most frequently documented possessors of tithe revenue in Silesia were canons of the cathedral chapter of Wrocław. The importance of the chapter is consistent with the grant of tithe revenues in the Polish duchies to the archbishop of Gniezno and presumably his suffragans in 1136. Thereafter, the impression of the importance of cathedral clergy may in part be an artifact of the documentation; most of the tithe grants are recorded by the bishops, who may have recorded transfers of those tithe revenues that had been possessed by members of their chapter more carefully than they did transfers of tithe revenues that had been possessed by someone else. However, Bishop Lawrence did record transfers of tithes by knights according to "knightly privilege," while Duke Henry acknowledged the bishops and chapter as the formal transferors of tithe revenue, and as its most important possessors. The importance of cathedral canons as possessors of tithe revenue is confirmed by the importance of the settlement from which they drew that revenue. Prebends of cathedral canons included tithe revenue from places included in some of the more important parishes in central Silesia.

The process of transfer of tithe revenue and definition of status of local churches centered largely on the cathedral chapter. The dynamics of that process shed light on the definition of the chapter as a corporate entity, on the balance of authority and initiative between bishop, chapter, and individual canons in disposing the prebends of the canons, and on the political and informal interrelationship between the chapter and the clergy outside it. In a formal sense, the chapter clearly acted as a corporate body through its expression of consent by its "senior and major part," through the presence of at least a group of officials of the chapter at the alienations, and through use of a seal. However, in practice consent of individual canons to alienations of their prebends, and perhaps to alienation of tithe revenue of the chapter as a whole, was important, and posed serious complications if it was in doubt. The conflict between Abbot Witosław and the cathedral canons Bogusław and Radulf spanning the years 1212 and 1220 suggests that once these complications arose, they were difficult to override by expression of formal consent of the bishop and chapter, existence of detailed written documentation, and use of seals. The ultimate results of that conflict, and the later conduct of Bishop Thomas, indicate that during the subsequent decades the power of the bishop in disposing of tithe revenue that had been part of a canon's prebend increased substantially. In addition to alienating tithe revenue, cathedral canons played a variety of formal and informal roles in such alienations, either for each other or for other clerics and laymen interested in alienating and acquiring tithes.[384]

As elsewhere in medieval Europe, the twelfth and thirteenth centuries witnessed a clear and sustained increase in the number of local churches that performed spiritual and pastoral functions. Throughout the period under study, parish churches were established in local and regional centers of economic and demographic expansion. Several parishes were formed in the town of Wrocław. Elsewhere, parish churches were situated in the most important localities within clusters of settlement. The resulting parishes

---

[384]The evidence on these issues is fragmentary, and rather hypothetical pending analogous study of chapters of other cathedral churches in a broader ecclesiastical context in other Polish duchies; but it does suggest the relationships among the clergy and their changes in one relatively well-documented ecclesiastical milieu.

were therefore not discrete villages, but local hierarchies of settlement and economic activity, consisting of central villages and their outliers. It is difficult to say whether this type of parish structure remained constant or changed over time, and if so when. There is no explicit evidence for formation of parishes at a level lower than the local center with its outliers during the period under study. However, Bishop Lawrence expected the appearance of such churches, and perhaps seigneurial churches and other churches licitly or illicitly constructed within the older large *parochiae* that serviced more local populations; but on the face of the record this society does not seem to have produced a church in every locality that had a place-name.

These reconstructions allow a tentative and localized estimate of the minimum density of the network of parishes in those relatively well-documented areas of central Silesia that were appropriated by the monastic communities in the early decades of the thirteenth century. In comparison to the distances between parish centers in several carefully studied regions of Europe, the distances between the parish centers were large. The distances between the parish centers of the *parochia* of the monks of Lubiąż, however, at least falls within a range familiar from other local studies. Similarly, on the one occasion when the size of the population inhabiting the parish of St. Peter's in Trzebnica can be estimated, the level, though modest, is also comparable to the population levels documented elsewhere.

These estimates are extremely conservative. They take into account only the parish churches appropriated by the major monastic communities at the outset of the century, within one relatively well-documented region of the diocese of Wrocław. They do not take account of local churches established under secular lordship, recurrently documented elsewhere as a routine if not typical parish church in the archdiocese of Gniezno as a whole. They also do not take into account any "daughter" churches licitly established within the large territories of the appropriated parishes around each *ecclesia matrix*, as Bishop Lawrence and others anticipated at the outset of the thirteenth century. Finally, they do not include the local churches that were established illicitly outside control of the major monastic communities in the course of the thirteenth century, and provoked conflicts between their patrons and the clergy that staffed them. The documentation suggests that the number of these additional churches was substantial, and that the contemporaries considered their construction as licit, ongoing parish expansion. Thus, an estimate of the total number of parish churches, of the geographic and demographic sizes of these churches, and of anything approaching a parish network, is based on very incomplete evidence for even the relatively well-documented region of earlier medieval Poland. Estimates of comparable quantitative figures for other, more sparsely documented regions of Silesia, for other localities, or, in some vague sense, for Poland as a whole, are a fortiori likely either very seriously to underestimate or distort the distribution of local churches in the Polish duchies, and complicate meaningful comparisons of thirteenth-century Poland or some region of it with other places.

A recurrent issue confronting the popes, legates, and bishops concerned with the archdiocese of Gniezno was control over the clergy which staffed the parish churches. Control was a subject of sharp conflict among several parties: secular landholders who possessed parish churches within their estates; the archbishop of Gniezno and his suffragans; and monastic communities that appropriated parishes. Because of the uneven and asymmetrical nature of the documentation, there is no way to assess the relative importance of each of these groups in anything remotely resembling quantitative proportions. However, the emphasis of the documents allows some insight into their relative importance within the archdiocese of Gniezno as a whole and within central Silesia. Reformers had stressed the need for supervision of local clergy by bishops, archdeacons, and archpriests, continuously since the first years of the thirteenth century; and instructed the local clergy to obey bishops and their agents as well as their secular patrons. At the outset of the century, the status of the local clergy and churches in question is ambiguously documented, but by the third decade the reforming canons clearly referred to parish clergy and parish churches, and thus assumed a network of each. Thus, at the level of the archdiocese as a whole, secular lords were the preeminent patrons of an expanding number of parish churches. At the level of the diocese of Wrocław, the evidence may be distorted by the unusually detailed documentation of the major monasteries in Silesia which appropriated parishes; nevertheless, it is clear that in this province regular clerics were important patrons of parish churches and their clergy. Ducal and seigneurial patronage is also documented, but not with the same frequency and level of detail.

This analysis helps situate the institutional, social, and economic history of Poland between the early twelfth and mid-thirteenth centuries in several broader contexts. One is the expansion of the economy, population, and lordship. Another is definition of statuses of the inhabitants of the Polish duchies, especially a gradual differentiation of two groups: knights and peasants. Between 1100 and 1250, each of these groups shifted towards a uniform legal status, economic privilege, economic obligation, and specialization.

A third context is the definition of ecclesiastical institutions at the turn of the twelfth and thirteenth centuries and thereafter, including the relationship between bishop and chapter, the degree of definition of the chapter as a corporate identity, the subdivision of large units of spiritual authority around older and central churches into more local and formally dependent parish churches, and control over all these processes by ecclesiastics and laymen. During the thirteenth century, we glimpse in this society a combination of strong and growing power of the bishop, strong power of the individual canons and rather weakly articulated corporate identity of the chapter, strong control over local churches and their revenues by lay patrons and bishops, weakening control over them by monastic patrons, and records of large, multi-settlement parishes in possession of the latter. Perhaps the closeness of episcopal and secular control explains both the demographic profile of Polish parishes and their overall modest number towards the end of the Middle Ages more accurately than semi-articulated models of arrested or delayed development.[385]

The materials also shed light on the dynamics of reform in a region of Europe expressly perceived as distant and unfamiliar by the contemporaries. Selection of concerns from the broad agenda of ecumenical councils for regional application, interpretations and adaptations of norms and refinement of remedies in light of regional usage, and recurrent balances of accommodation and prohibition, all illustrate the operation of canon law and its rules within a region of Europe and the significance of regional conditions for its refinement and implementation. The frequent recognition of the society within which that law was intended to operate as distant from the centers that periodically formulated it situates the Polish duchies meaningfully among the "frontier" regions of the contemporary European mental map. Finally, therefore, inquiry into tithes and parishes in their social context offers insight into legal, economic, institutional, and cultural integration of medieval Europe.

---

[385]See Morris, *Papal Monarchy*, 498, noting that in 1250 "in Poland it was still quite common to have ten or twenty villages associated with a mother church."

BIBLIOGRAPHY

SOURCE COLLECTIONS

A.P. Krzyżanowski, Stanisław, ed. *Album palaeographicum*. Kraków: Universitatis Iagellonicae sumptibus, 1959–60.

K.H. Grodecki, Roman, ed. and trans. *Księga henrykowska: Liber fundationis claustri sancte Marie Virginis in Heinrichow*. Poznań and Wrocław: Instytut Zachodni, 1949.

K.Maz. Korwin-Kochanowski, Jan Konrad, ed. *Codex diplomaticus et commemorationum Masoviae. Zbiór ogólny przywilejów i spominków mazowieckich*. Warsaw: Towarzystwo Naukowe Warszawskie, 1919.

K.Mp. Franciszek Piekosiński, ed. *Kodeks dyplomatyczny Małopolski*. Kraków: Akademia Umiejętności, 1876–86, repr. New York: Johnson Reprint Corporation, 1965.

K.Wp. Zakrzewski, Ignacy, and Franciszek Piekosiński, eds. *Kodeks dyplomatyczny Wielkopolski*. Poznań: Poznańskie Towarzystwo Przyjaciół Nauk, 1877–1908.

M.P.H. Bielowski, August, gen. ed. *Monumenta Poloniae Historica. Pomniki dziejowe Polski*. Lwów and Kraków: Akademia Umiejętności, 1864–93, repr. Warsaw: Państwowe Wydawnictwo Naukowe, 1960–61.

M.P.H., s.n. *Monumenta Poloniae Historica: Series Nova. Pomniki dziejowe Polski: Seria II*. Kraków: Polska Akademia Umiejętności, 1946–51, and Warsaw: Państwowe Wydawnictwo Naukowe, 1952–.

S.U., 1 Appelt, Heinrich, ed. *Schlesisches Urkundenbuch*, vol. 1: fascicle 1. Vienna, Cologne, and Graz: Hermann Böhlau, 1963; fascicle 2. Vienna, Cologne, and Graz: Hermann Böhlau, 1968; fascicle 3. Vienna, Cologne, and Graz: Hermann Böhlau, 1971.

S.U., 2 Irgang, Winfried, ed. *Schlesisches Urkundenbuch*, vol. 2. Vienna, Cologne, and Graz: Hermann Böhlau, 1978.

S.U., 3   Irgang, Winfried, ed. *Schlesisches Urkundenbuch*, vol. 3. Vienna, Cologne, and Graz: Hermann Böhlau, 1984.

V.-W.   Vrtel-Wierczyński, Stefan. *Wybór tekstów staropol-skich: czasy najdawniejsze do roku 1543* [A selection of Old Polish texts: the earliest times through the year 1543]. 4th ed., Warsaw: Państwowe Wy-dawnicto Naukowe, 1969.

SECONDARY SOURCES

Arnold, Benjamin. *German Knighthood, 1050–1300*. Oxford: Oxford University Press, 1985.

Aubin, Hermann. "Medieval Agrarian Society at its Prime: The Lands East of the Elbe and German Colonisation Eastwards." In Michael M. Postan, ed. *The Cambridge Economic History of Europe*, 2nd ed., 1:449–86. Cambridge: Cambridge University Press, 1966.

Aubrun, Michel. *La paroisse en France des origines au XVᵉ siècle*. Paris: Armand Collin, 1986.

Avril, Joseph. "A propos du proprius sacerdos: quelques ré-flexions sur les pouvoir du prêtre de paroisse." In *Proceedings of the Fifth International Congress of Medieval Canon Law*. Vatican City, 1980. Pp. 471–86.

———. "Paroisses et dépendances monastiques au moyen âge." In *Sous la Règle de Saint Benoît: structures monastiques et sociétés en France du moyen âge à l'époque moderne*. Geneva, 1982. Pp. 95–106.

———. "Recherches sur la politique paroissiale des établisse-ments monastiques et canoniaux (XIᵉ–XIIIᵉ siècles)," *Revue Mabillon*, 59 (1980): 453–513.

Barker, Graeme. *Prehistoric Farming*. Cambridge: Cambridge Uni-versity Press, 1983.

Barraclough, Geoffrey, ed. *Eastern and Western Europe in the Middle Ages*. London: Thames and Hudson, 1970.

Bartlett, Robert and Angus MacKay, eds. *Medieval Frontier So-cieties*. Oxford: Oxford University Press, 1989.

Berlière, Ursmer. "L'exercice du ministère paroissial par les moines dans le haut moyen âge," *Revue Mabillon*, 39 (1927): 227–50

Bettey, J. H. *Church and Parish: An Introduction for Local Historians*. London, 1987.

Bieniak, Janusz. "Rody rycerskie jako czynnik struktury społecznej w Polsce XIII–XIV wieku (Uwagi problemowe)" [Knightly kindreds as a factor of the the the social structure in Poland in the thirteenth and fourteenth centuries: Remarks on the issues], in Henryk Łowmiański, ed. *Polska w okresie rozdrobnienia feudalnego* [Poland in the period of feudal fragmentation]. Wrocław: Ossolineum, 1973. Pp. 161–200

Blair, John, ed. *Minsters and Parish Churches: The Local Church in Transition, 940–1200.* Oxford: Oxford University Press, 1985.

Bloch, Marc. *Feudal Society,* trans. L. A. Manyon. Chicago: University of Chicago Press, 1961.

Boyd, Catherine E. *Tithes and Parishes in Medieval Italy: The Historical Roots of a Modern Problem.* Ithaca: Cornell University Press, 1952.

Brooke, Christopher. "Rural Ecclesiastical Institutions in England: The Search for Their Origins," *Settimane di studio del Centro italiano di studi sull'alto medioevo,* 28 (1982): 685–711.

Brundage, James A. *Law, Sex, and Christian Society in Medieval Europe* Chicago: University of Chicago Press, 1987.

———— . "Tithes," *Dictionary of the Middle Ages,* 12:62–65

Buczek, Karol. "O chłopach w Polsce piastowskiej" [The peasants in Piast Poland], part 1, *Roczniki Historyczne,* 40 (1974): 50–105.

Burns, Robert I. *The Crusader Kingdom of Valencia: Reconstruction on a Thirteenth-Century Frontier.* Cambridge, Mass.: Harvard University Press, 1967.

———— . "The Significance of the Frontier in the Middle Ages." In Bartlett and MacKay, *Medieval Frontier Societies,* pp. 307–30.

Bynum, Caroline Walker. *Docere Verbo et Exemplo: An Aspect of Twelfth-Century Spirituality* (Harvard Theological Studies, No. 31). Missoula, Mont.: Scholars Press, 1979.

Cetwiński, Marek. *Rycerswo śląskie do końca XIII wieku: pochodzenie, gospodarka, polityka* [Silesian knighthood through the end of the thirteenth century: origins, economy, politics]. Wrocław: Ossolineum, 1980.

———— . *Rycerswo śląskie do końca XIII wieku: biogramy i rodowody* [Silesian knighthood through the end of the thirteenth century: biograms and genealogies]. Wrocław: Ossolineum, 1982.

Cieśla, Irena [same author as Irena Rabęcka and Irena Rabęcka-Brykczyńska]. "Taberna wczesnośredniowieczna na ziemiach polskich" [The early medieval tavern in Poland], *Studia Wczesnośredniowieczne,* 4 (1958): 159–225.

Constable, Giles. *Monastic Tithes from their Origins to the Twelfth Century.* Cambridge: Cambridge University Press, 1964.

————. "Monastic Rural Churches and the *cura animarum* in the Early Middle Ages," *Settimane di studio del Centro italiano di studi sull'alto medioevo,* 28 (1982): 349–89.

Coste, Jean. "L'institution paroissiale à la fin du moyen âge: approche bibliographique en vue d'enquêtes possibles," *Mélanges de l'école française de Rome,* 96 (1984): 295–326.

Darby, H. C. *Domesday England.* Cambridge: Cambridge University Press, 1977.

Davies, Norman. *God's Playground: A History of Poland.* 2 vols. New York: Columbia University Press, 1982.

Davies, Wendy. *Small Worlds: The Village Community in Early Medieval Brittany.* Berkeley and Los Angeles: University of California Press, 1988.

Devailly, Guy. "Le clergé régulier et le ministère paroissial," *Cahiers d'histoire,* 20 (1975): 259–72

Domański, Józef. *Nazwy miejscowe dzisiejszego Wrocławia i dawnego okregu wrocławskiego* [Place-names of today's Wroclaw and the former district of Wrocław]. Warsaw: Państwowe Wydawnictwo Naukowe, 1967.

Dowiat, Jerzy. *Chrzest Polski* [The baptism of Poland]. Warsaw: Państwowe Wydawnictwo Naukowe, 1969.

Duby, Georges. *La société aux XIe et XIIe siècles dans la région mâconnaise.* 2nd ed. Paris: S.E.V.P.E.N., 1971.

————. *Rural Economy and Country Life in the Medieval West,* trans. Cynthia Postan. Columbia, S.C.: University of South Carolina Press, 1968.

————. "The Nobility of Medieval France." In Georges Duby, *Chivalrous Society,* trans. Cynthia Postan. Berkeley and Los Angeles: University of California Press, 1977. Pp. 94–111.

Duggan, Lawrence G. *Bishop and Chapter: The Governance of the Bishopric of Speyer to 1552.* New Brunswick, N.J.: Rutgers University Press, 1978.

Dvornik, Francis. *The Slavs in European History and Civilization.* New Brunswick, N.J.: Rutgers University Press, 1962.

Fossier, Robert. *La terre et les hommes en Picardie jusqu'à la fin de XIIIe siècle.* Paris and Louvain: R. Nauwelaerts, 1968.

————. *Enfance de l'Europe, X^e–XIIe siècles: aspects économiques et sociaux.* 2 vols. Paris: Presses Universitaires de France, 1982.

————. "Le mise en place du cadre paroissial et l'évolution du peuplement," *Settimane di studio del Centro italiano di studi sull'alto medioevo,* 28 (1982): 495–563.

Freed, John B. "Nobles, Ministeriales and Knights in the Archdiocese of Salzburg," *Speculum,* 62 (1987): 575–611.

Fügedi, Eric. *Castle and Society in Medieval Hungary.* Budapest: Akadémiai Kiadó, 1986.

Gieysztor, Aleksander. "En Pologne médiévale: problèmes du régime politique et de l'organisation administrative du Xe au XIIIe siècles," *Annali della fondazione Italiana per la storia amministrativa,* 1 (1964): 135–56.

―――. "Le fonctionnement des institutions ecclésiastiques rurales en Bohême, en Pologne et en Hongrie aux Xe et XIe siècles," *Settimane di Studio del Centro italiano di studi sull'alto medioevo,* 28 (1982): 927–45.

―――, ed. *History of Poland.* 2d ed. Warsaw: Państwowe Wydawnictwo Naukowe, 1979.

Górecki, Piotr. "Economy, Society, and Lordship in Early Medieval Poland." Ph.D. Dissertation, University of Chicago, 1988.

―――. *Economy, Society, and Lordship in Medieval Poland, 1100–1250.* New York: Holmes and Meier, 1992.

―――. "Politics of the Legal Process in Early Medieval Poland," *Oxford Slavonic Papers, New Series,* 17 (1984): 23–44.

―――. "*Viator* to *ascriptitius:* Rural Economy, Lordship, and the Origins of Serfdom in Medieval Poland," *Slavic Review,* 42 (1983): 14–35.

Gottschalk, Joseph. *St. Hedwig, Herzogin von Schlesien.* Cologne and Graz: Hermann Böhlau, 1964.

Grabski, Andrzej Feliks. *Polska w opiniach Europy Zachodniej, XIV–XV w.* [Poland in Western European opinion in the fourteenth and fifteenth centuries]. Warsaw: Państwowe Wydawnictwo Naukowe, 1968.

Grüger, Heinrich. *Heinrichau: Geschichte eines schlesischen Zisterzienserklosters, 1227–1977.* Cologne and Vienna: Hermann Böhlau, 1978.

―――. "Das Volkstum der Bevölkerung in den Dörfern des Zisterzienserklosters Heinrichau im mittelschlesichen Vorgebirgslande vom 13.–15. Jahrhunderts," *Zeitschrift für Ostforschung,* 27 (1977): 241–61.

Halecki, Oskar. *A History of Poland.* New York: Roy Publishers, 1943.

Harvey, Sally. "The Knight and the Knight's Fee in England." In Rodney Hilton, ed. *Peasants, Knights and Heretics: Studies in Medieval English Social History.* Cambridge: Cambridge University Press, 1976. Pp. 133–76.

Heck, Roman. "The Main Lines of Development of Silesian Medieval Historiography," *Quaestiones Medii Aevi,* 2 (1981): 63–87.

Helmholz, Richard. "Canonists and Standards of Impartiality for Papal Judges Delegate." In Richard Helmholz, *Canon Law and the Law of England*. London: Hambledon Press, 1987. Pp. 21–40.

Hodges, Richard. *Dark Age Economics: The Origins of Towns and Trade, A.D. 500–1000*. New York: St. Martin's Press, 1982.

Hoffmann, Richard C. *Land, Liberties, and Lordship in a Late Medieval Countryside: Agrarian Structures and Change in the Duchy of Wrocław*. Philadelphia: University of Pennsylvania Press, 1989.

Hollister, C. Warren. *The Military Organization of Norman England*. Oxford: Oxford University Press, 1965.

Kłoczowski, Jerzy. *Dominikanie polscy na Śląsku w XIII–XIV wieku* [Polish Dominicans in Silesia in the thirteenth–fourteenth centuries]. Lublin: Wydawnictwo Katolickiego Uniwersytetu Lubelskiego, 1956.

——— . "Dominicans of the Polish Province in the Middle Ages." In Jerzy Kłoczowski, ed. *Christian Community in Medieval Poland*. Wrocław: Ossolineum, 1981. Pp. 73–118

——— . *Europa słowiańska w XIV–XV wieku* [Slavic Europe in the fourteenth and fifteenth centuries]. Warsaw: Państwowy Instytut Wydawniczy, 1984.

——— , ed. *Kościół w Polsce* [The Church in Poland]. 4 vols. Kraków: Znak, 1966.

Knoll, Paul. "Economic and Political Institutions on the Polish-German Frontier in the Middle Ages: Action, Reaction, Interaction." In Bartlett and MacKay, *Medieval Frontier Societies*, pp. 151–76

——— . *The Rise of the Polish Monarchy: Piast Poland in East Central Europe, 1320–1370*. Chicago: University of Chicago Press, 1972.

Koebner, Richard. "The Settlement and Colonisation of Europe." In Postan, *Cambridge Economic History*, 1:1–91.

Korta, Wacław. *Rozwój wielkiej własności feudalnej na Śląsku do połowy XIII wieku* [The development of feudal great property in Silesia until the mid-thirteenth century]. Wrocław: Ossolineum, 1964.

Kossmann, Oskar. *Polen im Mittelalter: Beiträge zur Sozial- und Verfassungsgeschichte*. Marburg/Lahn: J. G. Herder–Institut, 1971.

——— . *Polen im Mittelalter: Staat, Gesellschaft, Wirtschaft im Bannkreis des Westens*. Marburg/Lahn: J. G. Herder–Institut, 1985.

Kozłowska-Budkowa, Zofia. "Przyczynki do krytyki dokumentów śląskich z pierwszej połowy XIII wieku" [Contributions to source criticism of the Silesian documents from the first half of the thirteenth century]. In *Studia z historii społecznej i gospodarczej poświęcone Franciszkowi Bujakowi*. Lwów: Towarzystwo Naukowe, 1931. Pp. 1–6

Kürbis, Brygida. "Pogranicze Wielkopolski i Kujaw w X–XII wieku" [The borderlands of Great Poland and Cuiavia in the eleventh and twelfth centuries], in Czesław Łuczak (ed.), *Studia z dziejów ziemi mogileńskiej*. Poznań: Wydawnictwo Uniwersytetu Adama Mickiewicza, 1978. Pp. 65–111.

Kuhn, Walter. *Beiträge zur schlesischen Siedlungsgeschichte*. Munich: Delp, 1971.

———— . "Kastellaneigrentzen und Zehntgrenzen in Schlesien," *Zeitschrift für Ostforschung*, 21 (1972): 201–47.

———— . *Neue Beiträge zur schlesischen Siedlungsgeschichte: Eine Aufsatzsammlung*. Siegmaringen: Jan Thorbecke, 1984.

———— . *Siedlungsgeschichte Oberschlesiens*. Würzburg, 1954.

Kula, Witold. *Measures and Men*, trans. R. Szreter. Princeton: Princeton University Press, 1986.

Kumor, Bolesław and Zdzisław Obertyński, eds. *Historia Kościoła w Polsce* [History of the Church in Poland], vol. 1, part 1. Poznań and Warsaw: Palottinum, 1974.

Langdon, John. *Horses, Oxen, and Technological Innovation: The Use of Draught Animals in English Farming from 1066–1500*. Cambridge: Cambridge University Press, 1986.

Lea, Henry Charles. *A History of the Inquisition of the Middle Ages*, 3 vols. New York: Harper and Brothers, 1888; repr. New York: Russell and Russell, 1955.

Litak, Stanisław. "Rise and Spatial Growth of the Parish Organization in the Area of Łuków District in the Twelfth to Sixteenth Centuries." In Kłoczowski, *Christian Community*, pp. 149–81.

Lotter, Friedrich. "The Crusading Idea and the Conquest of the Region East of the Elbe." In Bartlett and MacKay, *Medieval Frontier Societies*, pp. 267–306.

Łowmiański, Henryk. *Początki Polski* [The origins of Poland]. 6 vols. Warsaw: Państwowe Wydawnictwo Naukowe, 1963–73.

———— . *Religia Słowian i jej upadek (w. VI–XII)* [The religion of the Slavs and its decline (seventh–twelfth centuries)]. Warsaw: Państwowe Wydawnictwo Naukowe, 1979.

Mączak, Antoni, Henryk Samsonowicz, and Peter Burke, eds. *East-Central Europe in Transition: From the Fourteenth to the Seventeenth Century*. Cambridge: Cambridge University Press, and Paris: Editions de la Maison des Sciences de l'Homme, 1985.

Maleczyński, Karol. *Dyplomatyka wieków średnich* [Medieval diplomatics]. Warsaw: Państwowe Wydawnictwo Naukowe, 1971.

———— . *Studia nad dokumentem polskim* [Studies on the Polish document]. Wrocław: Ossolineum, 1971.

Matuszewski, Józef. *Najstarsze polskie zdanie prozaiczne: zdanie henrykowskie i jego tło historyczne* [The oldest Polish sentence in prose: the sentence of Henryków and its historical background]. Wrocław: Ossolineum, 1981.

Menzel, Josef Joachim. *Die schlesischen Lokationsurkunden des 13. Jahrhunderts*. Würzburg: Holzner Verlag, 1977.

Młynarska-Kaletynowa, Marta. *Wrocław w XII–XIII wieku: przemiany społeczne i osadnicze* [Wrocław in the twelfth and thirteenth centuries: social and settlement changes]. Wrocław: Ossolineum, 1986.

Modzelewski, Karol. *Chłopi w monarchii wczesnopiastowskiej* [The peasants in the early Piast monarchy]. Wrocław: Ossolineum, 1987.

———— . "Jurysdykcja kasztelańska i pobór danin prawa książęcego w świetle dokumentów XIII w." [The castellan's jurisdiction and the collection of taxes due according to ducal law in light of thirteenth-century documents], *Kwartalnik Historyczny*, 87 (1980): 149–73.

———— . *Organizacja gospodarcza państwa piastowskiego, X–XIII wiek* [The economic organization of the Piast state between the tenth and thirteenth centuries]. Wrocław: Ossolineum, 1975.

Morris, Colin. *The Papal Monarchy: The Western Church from 1050 to 1250*. Oxford: Oxford University Press, 1989.

Mularczyk, Jerzy. *Władza książęca na Śląsku w XIII wieku* [Ducal power in Silesia in the thirteenth century]. Wrocław: Ossolineum, 1984.

Musset, Lucien. *Les invasions: le second assaut contre l'Europe chrétienne (V^e–XIe siècles)*. Paris: Presses Universitaires de France, 1965.

Nasiłowski, Kazimierz. "Samowolne migracje kleru w świetle polskiego prawa kościelnego przed soborem trydenckim" [Voluntary migrations of the clergy in light of the Polish ecclesiastical law before the Council of Trent], *Czasopismo Prawno-Historyczne*, 11 (1959): 9–38.

Płaza, Stanisław. *Źródła drukowane do dziejów wsi w dawnej Polsce: studium bibliograficzno-źródłoznawcze* [Printed sources for the history of the village in Old Poland: a bibliographic and source study]. Warsaw and Kraków: Nakladem Uniwersytetu Jagiellońskiego, 1974.

Rabęcka, Irena. "The Early Medieval Tavern in Poland," *Ergon*, 3 (1962): 372–75

Rabęcka-Brykczyńska, Irena and Franciszek Sławski. "Karczma" [The tavern], *Słownik Starożytności Słowiańskich*, 2 (1964): 373–75

Reynolds, Susan. *Kingdoms and Communities in Western Europe, 900–1300*. Oxford: Oxford University Press, 1984.

Sayers, Jane. *Papal Judges Delegate in the Province of Canterbury, 1198–1254*. Oxford: Oxford University Press, 1971.

Schmid, Heinrich Felix. *Die rechtlichen Grundlagen der Pfarrorganisation auf westslavischen Boden und ihre Entwicklung während des Mittelalters*. Weimar, 1938.

Silnicki, Tadeusz. *Dzieje i ustrój Kościoła katolickiego na Śląsku do końca w. XIV* [The history and structure of the Catholic Church in Silesia through the end of the fourteenth century]. Warsaw: Państwowe Wydawnictwo Naukowe, 1953.

——— . "Kardynał legat Gwido, jego synod wrocławski w roku 1267 i statuty tego synodu" [Cardinal legate Guido, his Wrocław synod of 1267, and the statutes of this synod], in Silnicki, *Z dziejów Kościoła w Polsce: studia i szkice historyczne* [Fragments of the history of the Church in Poland: studies and historical sketches]. Warsaw: Państwowe Wydawnictwo Naukowe, 1960. Pp. 321–80.

——— . *Organizacja archidiakonatu w Polsce* [Organization of the archdeaconate in Poland]. Lwów: Towarzystwo Naukowe, 1927.

Somerville, Robert. "'Pope Clement in a Roman Synod' and Pastoral Work by Monks," *Monumenta Germaniae Historica, Schriften*, Bd. 33.II. Hanover: Hahnsche Buchhandlung, 1988. Pp. 151–56.

Southern, Richard. *Western Society and Church in the Middle Ages*. Harmondsworth: Penguin, 1970.

Sullivan, Richard E. "Parish," *Dictionary of the Middle Ages*, 9:411–17.

Sułowski, Zygmunt. "Początki Kościoła polskiego" [Beginnings of the Polish Church]. In Kłoczowski, *Kosciół*, 1:17–123.

Sweeney, James Ross. "Innocent III, Canon Law, and Papal Judges Delegate in Hungary." In James Ross Sweeney and Stanley Chodorow, eds. *Popes, Teachers, and Canon Law in the Middle Ages*. Ithaca: Cornell University Press, 1989. Pp. 26–52.

Szymański, Józef. "Biskupstwa polskie w wiekach średnich: organizacja i funkcje" [Polish dioceses in the Middle Ages: organization and functions]. In Kłoczowski, *Kosciół*, 1:127–236.

Tazbirowa, Julia. "Początki organizacji parafialnej w Polsce" [Origins of the parish organization in Poland], *Przegląd Historyczny*, 5 (1963): 369–86.

————. "W sprawie badań nad genezą organizacji parafialnej w Polsce" [Research on the origins of the parish organization in Poland], *Przegląd Historyczny*, 5 (1963): 85–92.

Thomas, Alfred. "Czech-German Relations as Reflected in Old Czech Literature." In Bartlett and MacKay, *Medieval Frontier Societies*, pp. 199–216.

Tierney, Brian. *Foundations of the Conciliar Theory: The Contribution of the Medieval Canonists from Gratian to the Great Schism*. Cambridge: Cambridge Univesity Press, 1955, repr. 1968.

Toubert, Pierre. *Les structures du Latium médiéval: le Latium méridional et la Sabine du IXe siècle à la fin du XIIe siècle*. Rome: École Française de Rome, 1973.

Tymieniecki, Kazimierz. *Smardowie polscy: studium z dziejów społeczno-gospodarczych wczesnego średniowiecza* [The Polish smards: a study in the socio-economic history of the early Middle Ages]. Poznań: Poznańskie Towarzystwo Przyjaciół Nauk, 1959.

Van Engen, John. "The Christian Middle Ages as a Historiographical Problem," *American Historical Review*, 91 (1986): 519–52.

————. *Rupert of Deutz*. Berkeley and Los Angeles: University of California Press, 1983.

Vauchez, André. *La sainteté en Occident aux derniers siècles du moyen âge d'après les procès de canonisation et les documents hagiographiques*. Rome: École Française de Rome, 1981.

Vetulani, Adam. *Statuty synodalne Henryka Kietlicza* [The synodal statutes of Henryk Kietlicz]. Kraków: Polska Akademia Umiejętności, 1938.

Wallace-Hadrill, J. M. *The Frankish Church*. Oxford: Oxford University Press, 1983.

Wasilewski, Tadeusz. "Poland's Administrative Structure in Early Piast Times," *Acta Poloniae Historica*, 44 (1981): 71–99.

Wąsowicz, Teresa. "Une légende silésienne: sainte Hedwige dans la tradition littéraire et iconographique du XIIIe siècle." In Pierre Gallais and Yves-Jean Riou, eds. *Mélanges René Crozet*, 2:1073–78. Poitiers: Société d'Études Médiévales, 1966.

Wędzki, Andrzej. "Wrocław," *Słownik Starożytności Słowiańskich*, 6:604–14.

Weinstein, Donald and Rudolph M. Bell. *Saints and Society: The Two Worlds of Western Christendom, 1000–1700*. Chicago: University of Chicago Press, 1982.

White, Lynn, Jr. *Medieval Technology and Social Change*. Oxford: Oxford University Press, 1962.

Wiśniowski, Eugeniusz. "Rozwój organizacji parafialnej w Polsce do czasów reformacji" [Development of the parish organization in Poland until the Reformation]. In Kłoczowski, *Kościół*, 1:237–372.

Wojciechowski, Zygmunt. *Prawo rycerskie w Polsce przed statutami Kazimierza Wielkiego* [The knightly law in Poland prior to the statutes of Casimir the Great]. Poznań: Poznańskie Towarzystwo Naukowe, 1928.

Zachorowski, Stanisław. *Rozwój i ustrój kapituł polskich w wiekach średnich* [Development and structure of the Polish chapters in the Middle Ages]. Kraków: Akademia Umiejętności, 1912.

INDEX